MACMILLAN
McGR...

Science

Lucy H. Daniel

Jay Hackett

Richard H. Moyer

JoAnne Vasquez

About the Cover

Chameleons are known as the masters of camouflage. They have the ability to change their skin color and patterns. Chameleons are slow-moving animals so they rely on protective coloration for defense. For protection, a chameleon might show bright colors, which often means "bad-tasting" or "poison" to predators. If this doesn't work, they may shift to a dull color and play dead.

INQUIRY **What else would you like to know about chameleons? Write your own question or questions to answer.**

Mc Graw Hill **Macmillan McGraw-Hill**

Program Authors

Dr. Lucy H. Daniel
Teacher, Consultant
Rutherford County Schools, North Carolina

Dr. Jay Hackett
Professor Emeritus of Earth Sciences
University of Northern Colorado

Dr. Richard H. Moyer
Professor of Science Education
University of Michigan-Dearborn

Dr. JoAnne Vasquez
Elementary Science Education Consultant
Mesa Public Schools, Arizona
NSTA Past President

Contributing Authors

Lucille Villegas Barrera, M.Ed.
Elementary Science Supervisor
Houston Independent School District
Houston, Texas

Mulugheta Teferi, M.A.
St. Louis Public Schools
St. Louis, Missouri

Dinah Zike, M.Ed.
Dinah Might Adventures LP
San Antonio, Texas

The features in this textbook entitled "Amazing Stories," as well as the unit openers, were developed in collaboration with the National Geographic Society's School Publishing Division.

Copyright © 2002 National Geographic Society. All rights reserved.

Students with print disabilities may be eligible to obtain an accessible, audio version of the pupil edition of this textbook. Please call Recording for the Blind & Dyslexic at 1-800-221-4792 for complete information.

The McGraw·Hill Companies

Published by Macmillan/McGraw-Hill, of McGraw-Hill Education, a division of The McGraw-Hill Companies, Inc., Two Penn Plaza, New York, New York 10121.

FOLDABLES is a trademark of The McGraw-Hill Companies, Inc.

Printed in the United States of America

ISBN 0-02-282608-4

2 3 4 5 6 7 8 9 058/043 09 08 07 06 05

Teacher Reviewers

Michelle Dunning
Birmingham, Alabama

Donna Bullock
Chandler, Arizona

Debra Allen
Davie, Florida

Lora Meade
Plantation, Florida

Roxanne Laird
Miami, Florida

Karen Gaudy
Satellite Beach, Florida

Stephanie Sirianni
Margate, Florida

Heidi Stephens
South Daytona, Florida

Rosanne Phillips
Miami, Florida

Brenda Crow
Miami, Florida

Kari Pingel
Pella, Iowa

Christie Jones
Springfield, Illinois

Diane Songer
Wabash, Indiana

Lee Arwood
Wabash, Indiana

Margarite Hart
Indianapolis, Indiana

Charlotte Bennett
Newburgh, Indiana

Donna Halverson
Evansville, Indiana

Stephanie Tanke
Crown Point, Indiana

Mindey LeMoine
Marquette, Michigan

Billie Bell
Grand View, Missouri

Charlotte Sharp
Greenville, North Carolina

Pat Shane
Chapel Hill, North Carolina

Karen Daniel
Chapel Hill, North Carolina

Linda Dow
Concord, North Carolina

Consultants

Dr. Carol Baskin
University of Kentucky
Lexington, KY

Dr. Joe W. Crim
University of Georgia
Athens, GA

Dr. Pradeep M. Dass
Appalachian State University
Boone, NC

Dr. Marie DiBerardino
Allegheny University of
Health Sciences
Philadelphia, PA

Dr. R. E. Duhrkopf
Baylor University
Waco, TX

Dr. Dennis L. Nelson
Montana State University
Bozeman, MT

Dr. Fred Sack
Ohio State University
Columbus, OH

Dr. Martin VanDyke
Denver, CO

Dr. E. Peter Volpe
Mercer University
Macon, GA

Consultants

Dr. Clarke Alexander
Skidaway Institute of
Oceanography
Savannah, GA

Dr. Suellen Cabe
Pembroke State University
Pembroke, NC

Dr. Thomas A. Davies
Texas A & M University
College Station, TX

Dr. Ed Geary
Geological Society of America
Boulder, CO

Dr. David C. Kopaska-Merkel
Geological Survey of Alabama
Tuscaloosa, AL

Consultants

Dr. Bonnie Buratti
Jet Propulsion Lab
Pasadena, CA

Dr. Shawn Carlson
Society of Amateur Scientists
San Diego, CA

Dr. Karen Kwitter
Williams College
Williamstown, MA

Dr. Steven Souza
Williamstown, MA

Dr. Joseph P. Straley
University of Kentucky
Lexington, KY

Dr. Thomas Troland
University of Kentucky
Lexington, KY

Dr. Josephine Davis Wallace
University of North Carolina
Charlotte, NC

Consultant for Primary Grades

Donna Harrell Lubcker
East Texas Baptist University
Marshall, TX

Teacher Reviewers (continued)

Beth Lewis
Wilmington, North Carolina

Cindy Hatchell
Wilmington, North Carolina

Cindy Kahler
Carrboro, North Carolina

Diane Leusky
Chapel Hill, North Carolina

Heather Sutton
Wilmington, North Carolina

Crystal Stephens
Valdese, North Carolina

Meg Millard
Chapel Hill, North Carolina

Patricia Underwood
Randleman, North Carolina

E. Joy Mermin
Chapel Hill, North Carolina

Yolanda Evans
Wilmington, North Carolina

Tim Gilbride
Pennsauken, New Jersey

Helene Reifowitz
Nesconset, New York

Tina Craig
Tulsa, Oklahoma

Deborah Harwell
Lawton, Oklahoma

Kathleen Conn
West Chester, Pennsylvania

Heath Renninger Zerbe
Tremont, Pennsylvania

Patricia Armillei
Holland, Pennsylvania

Sue Workman
Cedar City, Utah

Peg Jensen
Hartford, Wisconsin

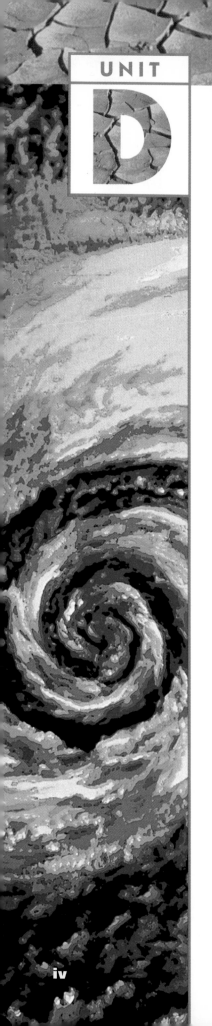

UNIT D

Earth Science

Astronomy, Weather, and Climate PAGE D1

For Your Reference

Science Handbook

Health Handbook

Activities

Unit D

Explore Activities

Quick Labs with FOLDABLES™

Inquiry Skill Builders

UNIT D

Astronomy, Weather, and Climate

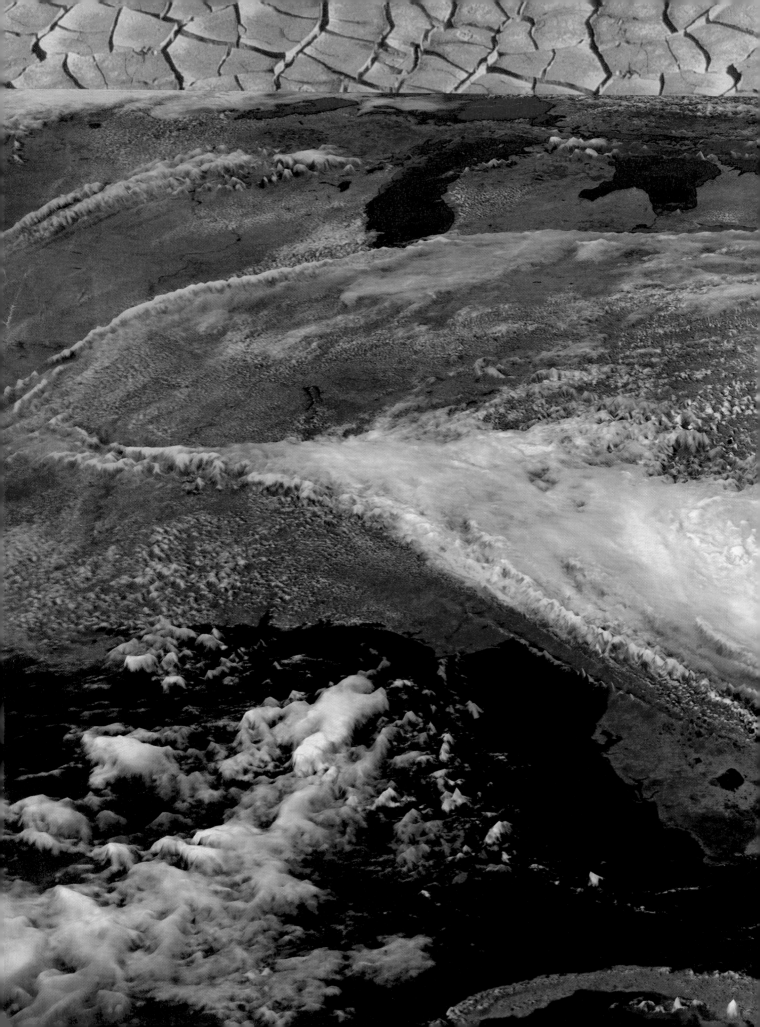

Astronomy, Weather, and Climate

LOOK!

A powerful hurricane swirls over the Atlantic Ocean. What causes such severe storms?

Astronomy

Did You Ever Wonder?

Did you ever see the clear night sky far from city lights? Did it ever seem to you that the stars formed patterns in the sky? Have you watched for one especially bright light that does not twinkle? A light that people call "the evening star"? It is not a star at all. It is the planet Venus. Venus and Earth are only two of many planets in our solar system. What are the other planets like?

INQUIRY SKILL Make a Model The Moon orbits Earth each month. Why does the Moon seem to change shape from night to night? Make a hypothesis. Design a model to test your hypothesis.

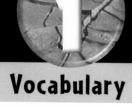

LESSON 1

Earth and Its Neighbors

Vocabulary

solar system, D6

planet, D6

gravity, D8

inertia, D8

revolve, D10

constellation, D12

Get Ready

Saturn is not standing still in one spot. It is moving around the Sun in an almost circular path. What holds Saturn, and all the other planets, near the Sun? What keeps each planet on its path?

Inquiry Skill

You use variables when you identify and separate things in an experiment that can be changed or controlled.

D 4

Explore Activity

How Are Earth and the Sun Held Together?

Materials

clay

string

scissors

meterstick

goggles

Procedure

BE CAREFUL! Wear goggles. Twirl the model close to the ground.

1. **Make a Model** Cut a 40-cm length of string. Wrap it around a small, round lump of clay in several directions. Tie the ends to make a tight knot. Measure 60 cm of string, and tie it to the string around the ball.

2. **Observe** Spin the ball of clay slowly—just fast enough to keep the string tight and the ball off the ground. Keep the ball close to the ground. Describe the path of the ball.

3. **Experiment** At one point while spinning, let the string go. What happens? Describe the path of the ball of clay. Repeat until you get a clear picture of what happens.

Drawing Conclusions

1. How did your model represent Earth and the Sun? What represented Earth? Where was the Sun located? How did you represent the force between them?

2. **Infer** Explain what happened when you let the string go. Why do you think this happened?

3. **FURTHER INQUIRY** **Use Variables** How would your results change if the mass of the clay were doubled? Tripled? How does the mass affect the pull on the string? Make a prediction. Try it.

Main Idea The solar system consists of nine planets, many moons, and many other bodies orbiting the Sun.

What Is the Solar System?

If you were traveling in a spaceship through space as fast as light, you would be passing stars. Perhaps in time you would approach one star in particular, the star you know as the Sun. If so, you would be approaching your home address, the **solar system**. The solar system is the Sun and the objects that are traveling around it.

Our Sun is an average-size star similar to many other stars in the night sky. It appears so large and bright to us because it is much closer to Earth. The Sun is composed mostly of hydrogen and helium. The formation of helium from hydrogen is what generates light and heat from the Sun.

The objects around the Sun include nine **planets**. Planets are objects that travel around a star in a path. That path is called an *orbit*. The planets are held in orbit around the Sun. The planets do not give off light, as stars do. They reflect light from their star, the Sun.

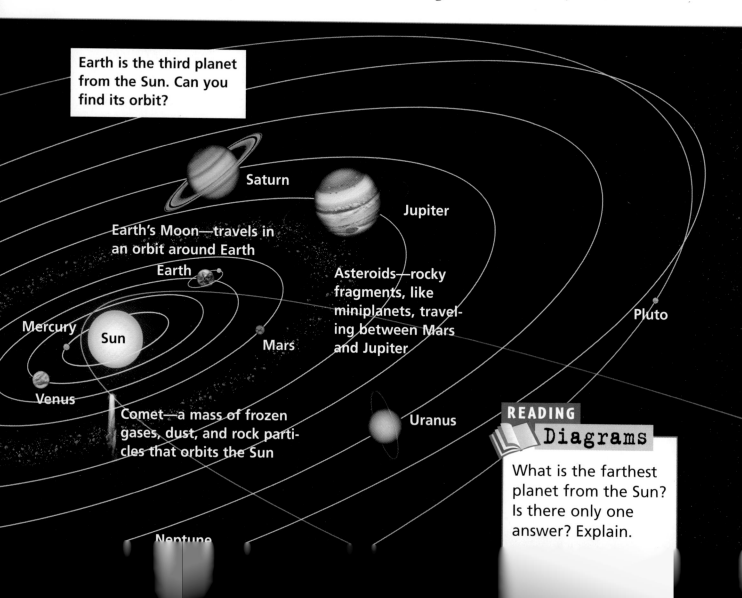

Earth is the third planet from the Sun. Can you find its orbit?

Saturn

Jupiter

Earth's Moon—travels in an orbit around Earth

Earth

Asteroids—rocky fragments, like miniplanets, traveling between Mars and Jupiter

Pluto

Mercury

Sun

Mars

Venus

Comet—a mass of frozen gases, dust, and rock particles that orbits the Sun

Uranus

Neptune

READING
Diagrams

What is the farthest planet from the Sun? Is there only one answer? Explain.

Except for Pluto, the orbit of each planet is almost a circle. Each orbit is slightly oval. What effect does an orbit of this shape have on the distance from a planet to the Sun?

One complete trip of an object in its orbit around the Sun takes one *year*. A year is different from planet to planet. For Earth one year is 365.25 days. The table shows how long a year takes for each planet. The time is given in days as days are timed on Earth.

▷ **What are the parts of the solar system?**

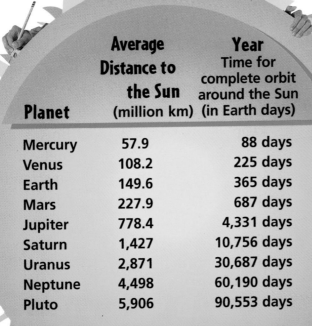

Planet	Average Distance to the Sun (million km)	Year Time for complete orbit around the Sun (in Earth days)
Mercury	57.9	88 days
Venus	108.2	225 days
Earth	149.6	365 days
Mars	227.9	687 days
Jupiter	778.4	4,331 days
Saturn	1,427	10,756 days
Uranus	2,871	30,687 days
Neptune	4,498	60,190 days
Pluto	5,906	90,553 days

QUICK LAB

Orbit Times

FOLDABLES Make a Folded Graph using graph paper as shown. (See p. R 41.)

1. **Communicate** Use graph paper to draw a bar graph to compare the revolution times for the planets. Tape the ends of the graph paper together to make an accordian graph. The horizontal axis represents time. Decide how much time each square represents. The vertical axis represents the planets. How many pieces of graph paper will you need?

2. **Interpret Data** What relationship can you find between the length of the year (time) and the planet's location in the solar system?

3. How could you change your graph to show the relationship even better? What might your new graph reveal?

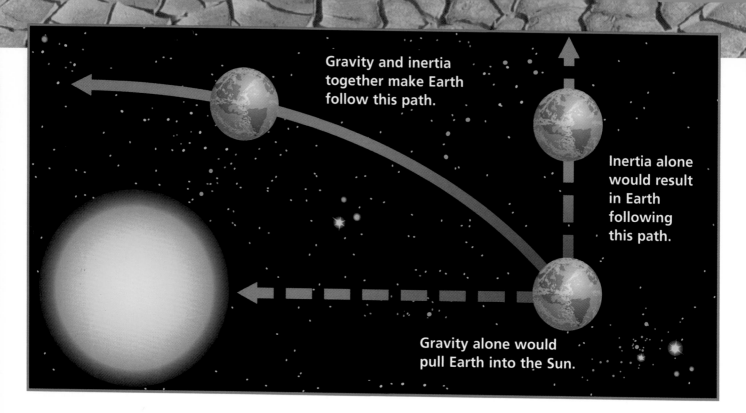

Gravity and inertia together make Earth follow this path.

Inertia alone would result in Earth following this path.

Gravity alone would pull Earth into the Sun.

What Keeps the Planets in Orbit?

The planets orbit the Sun, but what holds them in their paths? What keeps them from flying off into space?

Gravity

Over 300 years ago, Sir Isaac Newton described an invisible force holding the Sun and a planet together. He called the invisible force **gravity**. He described gravity as a property of all matter. It is a force of attraction, or pull, between any object and any other objects around it.

Gravity depends on two measurements—mass and distance. The more matter, or mass, in an object, the greater the pull in the object's direction. The closer two objects are, the stronger the pull of gravity between them.

The Sun has far more mass than any of the planets, so its gravity is much stronger, too. The Sun's gravity holds all of the objects in the solar system together. Without gravity, everything orbiting the Sun would go flying off into space.

Inertia

Gravity is not the only reason the planets stay in their orbits. Gravity alone would pull the planets into the Sun, because the Sun is so massive. That doesn't happen because the planets are moving. All objects—including the planets—have a property called **inertia** (i·NUR·shuh). Inertia is the tendency of a moving object to keep moving in a straight line.

Without gravity, the planets' inertia would keep them moving in straight lines. Gravity "steers" the planets in their oval paths around the Sun. Together, gravity and inertia keep the planets in their orbits.

READING Sequence of Events
How do gravity and inertia keep a planet in orbit?

What Makes a Day?

The Sun does more than just hold the planets in their orbits in the solar system. It also provides them with light and warmth. The Sun is the reason for day and night. All planets spin, or *rotate*, like huge spinning tops.

READING

Tables

Make a list of planets in order from the shortest day to the longest day.

Length of Day

Planet	Day = time for complete spin (in Earth hours or days)
Mercury	59 days
Venus	243 days
Earth	24 hours
Mars	24 hours 37 minutes
Jupiter	9 hours 56 minutes
Saturn	10 hours 40 minutes
Uranus	17 hours 14 minutes
Neptune	16 hours 7 minutes
Pluto	6.39 days

At any point in time, half of a planet is facing the Sun—it has daylight on that half. At the same time, half is facing away from the Sun—that half is in darkness, night.

As a planet rotates, places that are in darkness eventually turn to face the Sun, and those in daylight eventually turn away. Each planet makes one complete spin in its day. Each planet has its own speed of turning. The length of a day (that is, one complete day-night cycle) is different for each planet.

How much light and warmth a planet receives depends on how far it is from the Sun. Light spreads out as it travels outward from the Sun. An area of one square meter on the planet Mercury receives much more energy than an area of one square meter on a farther planet—such as Pluto. That is why Mercury is much hotter than Pluto.

 **What is a day?**

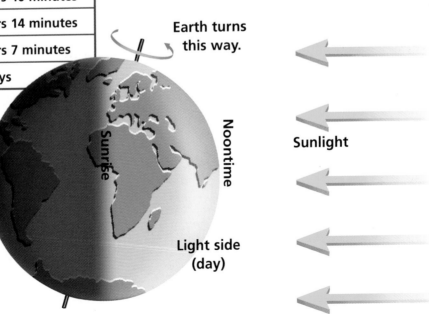

Earth turns this way.

Sunrise

Noontime

Sunlight

Dark side (night)

Light side (day)

What Is the Moon Like?

The Moon is Earth's nearest neighbor—"only" 384,000 km (240,000 mi) away. However, the Moon is not like Earth. There is no water to drink, no air to breathe. There is no weather, either. Without an atmosphere and oceans to trap and circulate heat, temperatures change greatly during a lunar day. With the Sun overhead, temperatures climb to over 123°C (253 °F). During a lunar night, temperatures can drop to -110°C (-170°F) or lower. At the Moon's shaded south pole, temperatures can drop to -233°C (-387°F).

The Moon has a rocky surface. With a telescope you can see its surface features. These include dark-colored regions called *maria* (MAHR·ee·uh). Maria is Latin for "seas." In the past, people thought these areas were oceans. The maria are really dry, flat land surrounded by mountains and ridges. Much of the Moon's surface is covered with huge dents, called craters. Some craters have trails of rock and dust extending out from them. The trails reflect sunlight and look like rays coming out of the crater.

At the same time Earth is **revolving**, or orbiting, around the Sun, the Moon is revolving around Earth. The Moon rotates on its axis once in the time it takes to orbit once around Earth. That means that the same side of the Moon is always facing Earth. However, the Moon seems to change shape, or phase, from day to day.

How Do Moon Phases Happen?

The light of the Moon comes from the Sun's rays striking it. Half of the Moon always faces the Sun, while the other half is in darkness. As the Moon travels around Earth we see different amounts of the lighted half. These are known as the Moon's phases. The phase we see depends on where the Moon is in relation to Earth and the Sun. It takes the Moon 29.5 days to complete all its phases.

▷ **How does the Moon differ from Earth?**

Earth's nearest neighbor looks nothing much like Earth.

Phases of the Moon

Third Quarter Moon

The Moon is three quarters of the way around Earth. This is sometimes called a half Moon.

Waning Crescent Moon

The left sliver of the Moon is the only part that you can see lighted.

Waning Gibbous Moon

As the Moon continues to move in its orbit, less of the lighted side is visible from Earth.

New Moon

The Moon is between the Sun and Earth.

The Moon is not visible in the sky.

Full Moon

Earth is between the Moon and the Sun.

The entire lighted side of the Moon is visible.

Waxing Crescent Moon

As the Moon moves in its orbit, more of the lighted side becomes visible from Earth.

Waxing Gibbous Moon

The gibbous Moon is almost full.

First Quarter Moon

The Moon is a quarter of the way around Earth. This is sometimes called a half Moon.

What Are Constellations?

When you look into the night sky, what else can you see besides the Moon? If the sky is dark enough, you can also see the stars. What are stars? A star is a large, hot ball of gas that is held together by gravity and gives off its own light. Stars look like points of light in the night sky. Unlike the Moon, stars are far outside the solar system.

In the past people looked at the stars and saw them arranged in groups that formed patterns in the sky. These patterns are called **constellations**. To these people the patterns looked like pictures of animals or people.

How can you find a star like Rigel in the night sky? The easiest way is by looking for its constellation. Rigel, for example, is a star in the constellation Orion, the hunter.

The pattern of stars in a constellation always looks the same even though the constellations appear to change position during the night and from season to season. As Earth travels in its orbit around the Sun, its night side faces different directions. You see only the constellations that are in that direction. For example, in the Northern Hemisphere, we see the constellation Orion in the winter months.

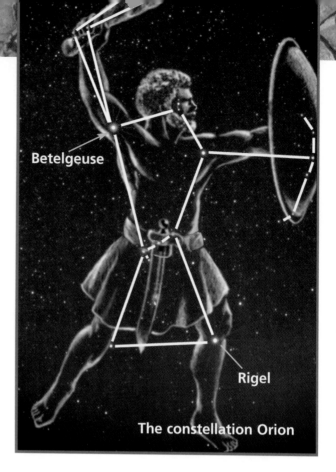

Betelgeuse

Rigel

The constellation Orion

▶ **Why do constellations appear to move across the sky?**

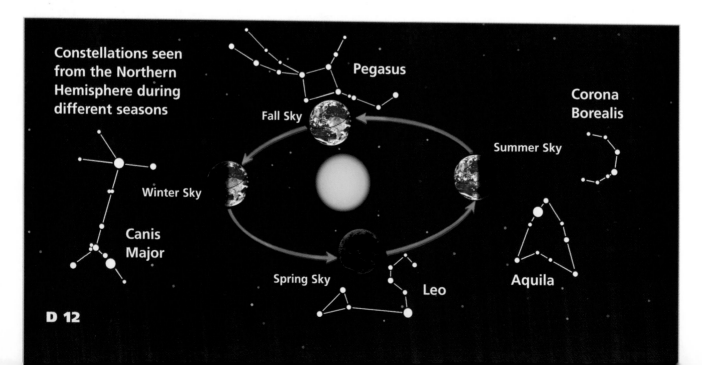

Constellations seen from the Northern Hemisphere during different seasons

Pegasus

Corona Borealis

Fall Sky

Summer Sky

Winter Sky

Canis Major

Spring Sky

Leo

Aquila

L·I·N·K·S

Why It Matters

Earth is teeming with life and movement. The Sun's energy helps produce seasons, day-to-day weather, and climates.

When astronauts first visited the Moon in 1969, they faced a tough problem. How do you survive in such a place? They had to bring all of the things they needed to stay alive all the way from Earth.

Earth is the only member of the solar system that supports life as we know it.

e-Journal Visit our Web site www.science.mmhschool.com to do a research project on the solar system.

Think and Write

1. How would you state your address in space? Explain your answer.

2. How is gravity important for Earth?

3. What keeps the planets in orbit around the Sun? Explain.

4. Why is the Moon unlivable compared with Earth?

5. **Critical Thinking** Would you weigh the same on the Sun as you do on Earth? Explain your answer.

MATH LINK

Estimate sizes. Stars come in different colors and sizes. Rigel is a blue supergiant with a diameter about 100 times larger than the Sun. Red supergiant Betelgeuse has a diameter about 1,000 times larger than the Sun. About how much larger is Betelgeuse than Rigel?

SOCIAL STUDIES LINK

Research the planets. Learn more about Earth's neighbors. Which planets have moons? Rings? Which planets are most likely to support life? Use the Internet or an encyclopedia.

WRITING LINK

Expository Writing How are telescopes used to magnify distant objects in the sky, such as the Moon and the planets? Use the Internet or an encyclopedia for your research. Write an essay about your findings.

TECHNOLOGY LINK

 LOG ON Visit www.science.mmhschool.com for more links.

The Solar System

Vocabulary

inner planet, D16

outer planet, D16

asteroid belt, D19

asteroid, D19

meteor, D19

meteorite, D19

comet, D19

galaxy, D20

Get Ready

This is an artist's idea of what a spaceprobe would look like as it passes one of Earth's neighbors. Do you know which planet this is? Even without a telescope you can see several planets during the year. How big is the solar system? How do the distances between planets compare? Construct a model to find out.

Inquiry Skills

You **make a model** when you make something to represent an object or an event.

Explore Activity

How Do the Distances Between Planets Compare?

Materials

roll of paper towels

markers

tape (optional)

ruler

Procedure

1 **Use Numbers** Study the chart. Distances are in Astronomical Units (A.U.). One A.U. is the distance from Earth to the Sun. How far from the Sun is Mars? Pluto?

Planet	Distance (A.U.)
Mercury	0.39
Venus	0.7
Earth	1.0
Mars	1.5
Jupiter	5.2
Saturn	9.5
Uranus	19.2
Neptune	30
Pluto	39.4

2 **Make a Model** Let the width of one paper towel be one A.U. Lay out the length of paper towels you need to show the distance from the Sun to Pluto. Measure and mark the location of each planet.

Drawing Conclusions

1 **Interpret Data** Describe how the planets are spaced.

2 **Use Numbers** It takes 8 minutes for light to travel from the Sun to Earth. How long does it take for light to travel to Jupiter? To Pluto?

3 **FURTHER INQUIRY** **Make a Model** Your model has all the planets lined up. Actually, the planets are scattered in different places in their orbits. How can you change your model to be more accurate? Make a plan and try it.

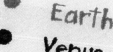

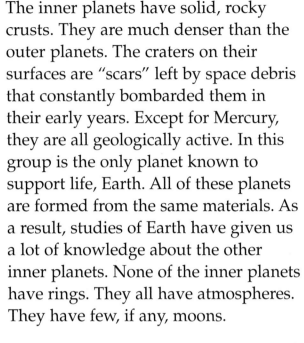

Main Idea Our solar system consists of four inner planets, five outer planets, moons, and other small bodies.

How Do the Inner Planets Compare?

The planets of our solar system can be divided into two groups. Those closest to the Sun are the **inner planets**. Those beyond the asteroid belt are the **outer planets**.

Small and warm, the inner planets are Mercury, Venus, Earth, and Mars.

The inner planets have solid, rocky crusts. They are much denser than the outer planets. The craters on their surfaces are "scars" left by space debris that constantly bombarded them in their early years. Except for Mercury, they are all geologically active. In this group is the only planet known to support life, Earth. All of these planets are formed from the same materials. As a result, studies of Earth have given us a lot of knowledge about the other inner planets. None of the inner planets have rings. They all have atmospheres. They have few, if any, moons.

Mercury
Mercury is the closest planet to the Sun and orbits the Sun in the shortest time. Mercury rotates three times on its axis for every two revolutions around the Sun. This results in extremely hot temperatures on one side of the planet and extremely cold temperatures on the other side. Mercury has no moons.

Venus
Venus is the hottest planet. Its dense cloud cover holds in the Sun's heat and the heat given off by its volcanoes. Temperatures on Venus reach 482°C (900°F) and surface pressures are high enough to crush spacecraft. Venus also rotates backwards, and a day on Venus is longer than its year. Venus has no moons.

Earth
Earth is the water planet. It is our home. It has the right temperatures and resources for life as we know it to exist. Earth has one Moon.

Mars
The largest volcano in our solar system, Olympus Mons, is found on Mars. Mars has a thin atmosphere, but has strong winds and pink dust storms. There may once have been liquid water on Mars' surface. From the surface of Mars, its two moons, Phobos and Deimos, seem to move in opposite directions. Swift Phobos rises in the west and sets in the east usually twice a Martian day.

 How does Venus compare to Earth?

Inquiry Skill BUILDER

Making a Model of the Solar System

In this activity you will make a model to compare the sizes of the planets in the solar system. The table "Comparing a Planet's Radius with Earth's" will tell you how the radius of each "model planet" you make would compare to your model of Earth.

Materials

construction paper

white paper

pencil

string 25 cm long

metric ruler

colored markers or colored pencils

tape

Procedure

1 **Use Numbers** Look at the table. How much bigger is Jupiter's radius than Earth's radius? How much smaller is Mars' radius than Earth's?

2 **Measure** Let your model Earth's radius be 1 cm. Using this scale, how big would you need to make the radius of Jupiter? How big would you need to make the radius of Mars?

Comparing a Planet's Radius with Earth's			
Planet	**Radius (in Earth radii)**	**Planet**	**Radius (in Earth radii)**
Mercury	0.38 x Earth	Jupiter	11.2 x Earth
Venus	0.95 x Earth	Saturn	9.5 x Earth
Earth	1 x Earth	Uranus	4.0 x Earth
Mars	0.53 x Earth	Neptune	3.9 x Earth
		Pluto	0.18 x Earth

3 **Make a Model** Draw a model Earth with a 1cm radius. Cut out your model. Repeat this process for each planet.

Drawing Conclusions

1 **Compare** Look at the sizes of your model planets. Which planets are almost the same size?

2 **Compare** The radius for Saturn and its rings is over 28.5 times Earth's radius. How much larger is that than Jupiter's radius?

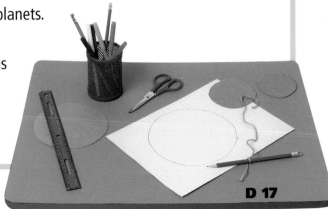

How Do the Outer Planets Compare?

Beyond the asteroid belt lie the outer planets. They are Jupiter, Saturn, Uranus, and Neptune—the gas giants— and tiny, icy Pluto. These planets formed in an area where temperatures were lower. This allowed lighter, less dense materials to clump together and form planets. The cores of the gas giants are dense and rocky. Surrounding the core of each planet are layers of dense liquids. Each gas giant is surrounded by large envelopes of gases. The gas giants also have rings. These range from the breathtaking rings of Saturn to the faint gray rings of Uranus. All of the outer planets have many moons, except for Pluto, which has only one. The period of revolution is much slower among the outer planets. The outer planets take many years to orbit the Sun. However, the gas giants rotate in a period of hours, not days.

Jupiter
The largest planet is the fastest spinner. A "day" on Jupiter is less than 10 hours long. Jupiter has a giant red spot—a storm—that has lasted over 300 years. Lightning bolts and auroras can be seen on Jupiter's night side.

Saturn
Find an ocean big enough and this "Lord of the Rings" would float! Giant Saturn is less dense than water! Saturn has the most visible and beautiful rings of all the planets. Saturn is almost twice as far from the Sun as Jupiter.

Between and Beyond the Planets

Between the orbits of Mars and Jupiter is the **asteroid belt**. Here, many small, rocky objects orbit the Sun. These are the **asteroids**. The largest asteroid, Ceres, is about one-fourth the diameter of Earth's Moon.

Pieces of space rock sometimes fall through Earth's atmosphere. Most of them burn up before they hit the ground. These are the "shooting stars," or **meteors**. Space rocks that reach the ground are called **meteorites**. Meteors can come from asteroids. They can also come from material left behind by **comets** as they orbit the Sun.

Comets are "dirty snowballs"— mixtures of ice, rock, and dust "left over" from the formation of the solar system. Beyond Neptune's orbit, 30 to 100 A.U. from the Sun, is the Kuiper Belt. *Short-period comets*—those that take less than 200 years to orbit the Sun—come from here. Beyond Pluto, about 100,000 A.U. from the Sun, is the Oort cloud. *Long-period comets*—those taking up to 30 million years to orbit the Sun—come from here.

What are comets made of? In January, 2004, the spacecraft *Stardust* flew past Comet Wild 2 and collected material from the comet. It also photographed what may be boulders, high cliffs, and impact craters on the comet's surface

Uranus
Uranus has been called "the planet that was knocked on its side." As a result of its tilt, its poles take turns pointing toward the Sun. Even so, Uranus is hotter at its equator, though scientists don't yet know why. Uranus is about twice as far from the Sun as Saturn. A day on Uranus is $17\frac{1}{4}$ hours long, but it takes 84 Earth-years to orbit the Sun. As springtime comes to Uranus, the planet shows that it has the brightest clouds in the outer solar system.

Neptune
Distant Neptune is almost 4.5 billion km from the Sun. Neptune's year is 165 Earth-years long, but its day is only about 16 hours long. Winds whip around Neptune at almost 1250 miles an hour (2000 km/hr).

Pluto
Tiny Pluto is farthest from the Sun. It is made up of frozen gases with lesser amounts of rocky materials. It is the only planet that has not yet been visited by spacecraft. Little is known about Pluto and its moon, Charon. There has even been some debate among astronomers over whether Pluto should be called a planet.

Are There Other Solar Systems?

Our Sun is only one of billions of stars in our own Milky Way **galaxy**. The Milky Way is only one of billions of star systems in the universe. Are there other Earth-like planets? Might some form of life exist elsewhere in the universe? Scientists are trying to find out.

So far, astronomers have discovered more than 100 giant planets orbiting other stars. These giant planets are more like Jupiter than like Earth. Does that mean there are no Earth-size planets elsewhere? No. It simply means small, Earth-size planets are much harder to detect.

In the next few years, scientists at NASA hope to launch a number of missions to look for planets around other stars. Two missions, in particular, will search for Earth-like planets. The first of those missions is *Kepler*, now scheduled to be launched in 2007. *Kepler* will study 100,000 sun-like stars. It will look for planets orbiting their stars at distances where liquid water could exist.

In 2013, NASA plans to launch the *Terrestrial Planet Finder*—a space telescope that will be able to find small, rocky planets orbiting other stars. The *Terrestrial Planet Finder* would also examine any atmospheres around those planets.

A possible future mission, *Life Finder*, would search such planets for seasonal changes in their atmospheres. It would also search for other changes that might indicate the presence of life.

▷ **Why is it harder to search for Earth-like planets than Jupiter-like planets orbiting other stars?**

Are there other Earth-like planets elsewhere in the galaxy? Astronomers are trying to find out.

L·I·N·K·S

Why It Matters

What was the early solar system like? Scientists hope to learn more when *Stardust* returns to Earth with its samples from Comet Wild 2. How likely are there to be Earth-like planets elsewhere in the universe? Scientists may find answers as they study distant solar systems. Might life forms exist on other worlds? Future space missions to Mars and to three of Jupiter's largest moons—which may have oceans below their icy crusts—may give us clues. They may also help us to remember how special our own planet Earth really is.

e-Journal Visit our Web site www.science.mmhschool.com to do a research project on space missions.

Think and Write

1. How do the inner planets compare with the outer planets?

2. Name one way Saturn differs from the other gas giants.

3. Name one thing that makes Uranus unusual.

4. INQUIRY SKILL **Make a Model** Model how our solar system might look from another star. (Hint: The Sun's radius is about 100 times Earth's.)

5. **Critical Thinking** Why is it so difficult to design a real-scale model of the solar system?

MATH LINK

Build a model solar system. The distance from Earth to the Sun (1 A.U.) is about 23,500 times the length of Earth's radius. If you let Earth's radius be one centimeter, about how far away would you have to place your model Pluto from your model Sun?

WRITING LINK

Writing That Compares What do all comets have in common? How do they differ? Compare Comet Hale-Bopp and Halley's Comet. Research both comets. List their similarities and differences in a Venn diagram. Use your Venn diagram to write an essay that compares and contrasts comets.

LITERATURE LINK

Read *2061: Photographing Mars* to learn about a teacher's trip to Mars. Try the activities at the end of the book.

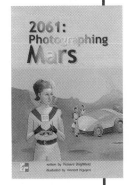

TECHNOLOGY LINK

 Visit www.science.mmhschool.com for more links.

PLANETARY WEATHER

What's the weather like on other planets? Knowing about the atmosphere on other planets tells us more about our entire solar system.

Over the years scientists have learned that Venus's atmosphere is 97 percent carbon dioxide. A greenhouse effect occurs when the layer of carbon dioxide traps the Sun's heat, making Venus's average temperature 460°C (860°F).

Like Earth, Jupiter has storms. The Sun heats our atmosphere which creates conditions that cause storms. But Jupiter receives less of the Sun's heat than Earth. Scientists believe that storms on Jupiter might originate with heat rising from the planet's own hot interior. When it rains on Jupiter it rains liquid helium!

Venus has yellow clouds of sulfuric acid. Precipitation from these clouds is like acid rain on Earth, only worse.

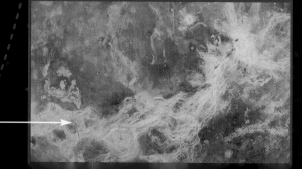

One of Jupiter's storms, the Great Red Spot, is about two times the size of Earth. It began before telescopes were invented.

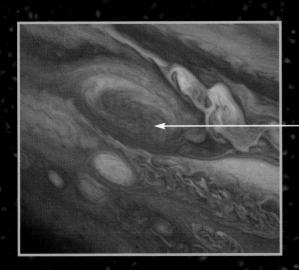

Saturn has three cloud layers—water clouds, ammonia clouds, and ammonium hydrosulfide clouds. Together they form smog!

There is lightning on Venus, Jupiter, and Saturn. Uranus and Neptune are believed to have lightning as well. The lightning is from electrical discharges. Flashes on Jupiter may be 500 kilometers (310 miles) across.

Pluto has the greatest atmospheric changes of all the planets. That's because its orbit is irregular.

When Pluto is at its closest position to the Sun, the heat turns the frozen nitrogen on Pluto into a gas. This gives Pluto an atmosphere and weather to go with it. As Pluto moves farther from the Sun, the gas freezes.

Write ABOUT IT

1. Why should the atmosphere on Venus be a warning to us on Earth?

2. What forms of weather do we share with other planets?

LOG ON Visit www.science.mmhschool.com to learn more about weather on other planets.

Chapter 9 Review

Vocabulary

Fill each blank with the best word or words from the list

comet, D19
constellation, D12
galaxy, D20
gravity, D8
inner planet, D16

meteor, D19
meteorite, D19
outer planet, D16
planet, D6
solar system, D6

1. The Sun and planets are part of the _____.

2. Earth is a(n) _____ that orbits the Sun.

3. The force of _____ keeps planets from flying off into space away from the Sun.

4. A planet between the Sun and the asteroid belt is called a(n)_____

5. A planet beyond the asteroid belt is known as a(n) _____.

6. Our Milky Way is a star system known as a(n)_____.

7. Stars that seem to form a pattern in the night sky are called a(n) _____.

8. A piece of space rock that burns up in the atmosphere is called a(n)_____.

9. A piece of space rock that survives its fall through the atmosphere and lands on the surface is called a(n)_____.

10. An object that comes from the Oort cloud is a(n)_____.

Test Prep

11. The Moon is unlivable compared with Earth because_____.

  A there is too much water

  B there is too much snow

  C there is too much smog

  D there is no air to breathe

12. The planet Saturn could _____.

  F fit inside Jupiter's Great Red Spot

  G fit in the Atlantic Ocean

  H float if there were an ocean big enough to hold it

  J fit inside the Grand Canyon

13. A year on Mercury is_____.

  A shorter than a year on Venus

  B longer than a year on Jupiter

  C the same as a year on Earth

  D the same as a year on Mars

14. A day on Venus is _____.

  F shorter than a day on Earth

  G shorter than a day on Mars

  H shorter than a day on Jupiter

  J longer than its year

15. Which planets have rings?

   A Mars, Jupiter, and Saturn

   B Saturn, Pluto, Neptune, and Venus

   C Jupiter, Saturn, Neptune, and Venus

   D Jupiter, Saturn, Uranus, and Neptune

Concepts and Skills

16. INQUIRY SKILL **Make a Model** Explain how you would model the distances between planets if you were using a football field and put your model Earth on the 2-yard line.

17. Critical Thinking Why is it difficult to find Earth-like planets elsewhere in the galaxy?

18. Reading in Science Explain the sequence of events that would happen if the force that keeps the planets orbiting the Sun did not exist.

19. Scientific Methods Design an experiment to show why Mercury gets much hotter than Pluto.

20. Decision Making What would you need to bring along on a space mission to another planet? Explain your choices.

Did You Ever Wonder?

INQUIRY SKILL **Infer** You want to send a spacecraft to visit each of the giant planets. What do you need to consider in planning your mission?

LOG ON Visit www.science.mmhschool.com to boost your test scores.

CHAPTER 10

Weather

Did You Ever Wonder?

What causes frost to form? Frost forms when it is cold enough for water vapor in the air to change from gas to ice crystals on grass and other objects. In warmer weather dew would form instead of frost.

INQUIRY SKILL Experiment Make frost in your classroom! Layer salt and ice in a metal container. Observe the outside of the container.

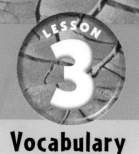
Atmosphere and Air Temperature

Vocabulary

insolation, D30
atmosphere, D32
troposphere, D32
air pressure, D33
weather, D34
barometer, D34

Get Ready

If it's summer, is it always hot? These animals may find it warmer in summer than in winter. However, it isn't exactly hot here on this beautiful summer day. How can summer be hot in some places and so cold in others?

How does the angle at which the Sun's energy hits Earth affect the warming of Earth?

Inquiry Skill

You experiment when you perform a test to support or disprove a hypothesis.

Explore Activity

Does the Sun's Angle Matter?

Materials

3 thermometers

triangular blocks

black paper

white paper

centimeter ruler

scissors

tape

150-W clear-bulb lamp

stopwatch

foam bowl

clay

Procedure

BE CAREFUL! Do not look into the lamplight.

1 Place a thermometer onto each of the three blocks, as shown. Cover each with black paper. Put the blocks 20 cm from the light bulb, level with its filament (curly wire).

2 **Observe** Measure the starting temperature at each block. Record the temperatures.

3 **Predict** What will happen when the lamp is turned on? Turn the lamp on. Record the temperature at each block every two minutes for ten minutes.

4 **Communicate** Make a line graph showing the change in temperature at each block over time.

5 **Use Variables** Repeat the activity with white paper.

Drawing Conclusions

1 **Communicate** Which block's surface was warmed most by the lamplight? Which block's surface was warmed the least?

2 **Infer** How does the angle at which light hits a surface affect how much the surface is heated? How does the surface color affect how much it is heated?

3 **FURTHER INQUIRY** **Experiment** What other factors might affect how much a surface is warmed by sunlight? How would you test your ideas?

Read to Learn

Main Idea The Sun warms Earth's surface, which transmits heat to the air above it.

Does the Sun's Angle Matter?

Where do you think you might find warm temperatures all year long? Where would you find very cold weather? That depends a lot on the angle at which sunlight hits a region. Angles make a difference in how much the Sun warms an area. The areas around the equator are hottest. That's because the Sun's path is high over-head at midday. In those areas the Sun's rays hit Earth at their strongest.

The areas around the North and South Poles are coldest. In those areas the Sun is much lower at midday.

The Sun's rays hit Earth's surface at a low angle. The strength of the rays is much weaker at this angle.

The angle at which sunlight strikes Earth's surface is called the angle of **insolation**. *Insolation* is short for *in*coming *sol*ar radi*ation*. It means the amount of the Sun's energy that reaches Earth at a given place and time.

The diagram shows how sunlight warms Earth in summer and winter. The amount of warming depends on the angle of insolation. The greater the angle, the warmer it gets. The angle of insolation is always smaller near the poles than near the equator. That means while it's freezing cold in one part of the world, it's hot in another.

▷ **How do differing angles of insolation cause differences in warming?**

How Sunlight Warms Earth

The Sun's rays strike the surface at different angles as Earth travels around the Sun.

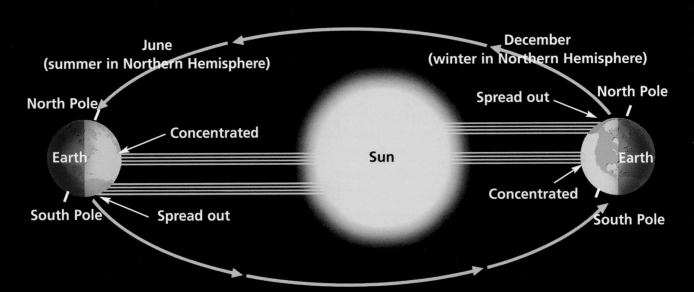

June (summer in Northern Hemisphere)

December (winter in Northern Hemisphere)

North Pole — Concentrated — Earth — South Pole — Spread out

Sun

Spread out — North Pole — Earth — Concentrated — South Pole

Angles count! Earth is actually closer to the Sun when it's winter in the Northern Hemisphere.

What Affects Insolation?

In the morning the Sun is close to the horizon. What happens as time goes by? At midday the Sun is high up in the sky, as high as it gets during the day. After midday the Sun is lower and lower in the sky.

How does this affect the angle of insolation? How do we measure it? Look at the shadows cast by objects they strike! The lower the angle of the light rays, the longer the shadows. As you can see in the diagram, the angle of insolation is the same as the angle between the ground and the line from the tip of the shadow to the top of the wall.

? How does the time of day affect the angle of insolation?

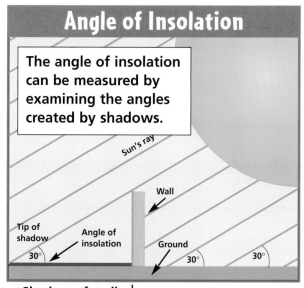

Angle of Insolation

The angle of insolation can be measured by examining the angles created by shadows.

Sun's ray

Wall

Tip of shadow

Angle of insolation

Ground

30°   30°   30°

◄Shadow of wall►|

READING
Diagrams

What will happen to the angle as the Sun gets higher in the sky? How will this affect the temperature?

QUICK LAB

Investigating Angles

FOLDABLES™ Make a Trifold Book. (See p. R 42.)

1. **Fold** a sheet of graph paper lengthwise in three equal parts. Put a small lump of clay in the middle of each part. Stand a toothpick straight up in each lump of clay.

2. **Hold** a flashlight directly over the first toothpick. Have a partner trace a line around the circle of light and trace the toothpick's shadow.

3. **Use Variables** Repeat step 2 for the other two toothpicks, changing only the angle of the flashlight.

4. **Measure** Count the number of boxes in each circle. Measure the lengths of the toothpick shadows. Record your results.

5. **Infer** Use the Trifold Book to record how the length of the shadow is related to the angle.

6. **Infer** Record how the number of boxes in the circle is related to the angle.

Why Do You Cool Down As You Go Up?

Did you ever climb a high mountain? As you go higher and higher above sea level, air temperatures drop. The natural drop in air temperature with altitude is about 2°C (3.6°F) for every 305 meters (1,000 ft).

Climbing up a mountain is really a journey up into the **atmosphere**, the air that surrounds Earth. The atmosphere reaches from Earth's surface to the edge of space. What if you could travel to the top part of the atmosphere? The diagram of the atmosphere shows what you would find.

You would find that the temperature does not fall steadily with altitude. It changes abruptly several times. These changes mark the boundaries of four main layers. These layers surround Earth like huge shells.

The layer closest to Earth's surface is the **troposphere** (TROP·uh·sfeer). It's the narrowest layer—between 8 and 18 kilometers (5–11 miles) thick—but it contains most of the air in the atmosphere. All life on Earth exists here. In this layer all moisture is found and all clouds, rain, snow, and thunderstorms form. Above this layer the air gradually thins out to the near-emptiness of space, with no exact upper boundary.

READING
Diagrams

Describe how the temperature changes in each layer of the atmosphere.

> **What is the relationship between altitude and temperature?**

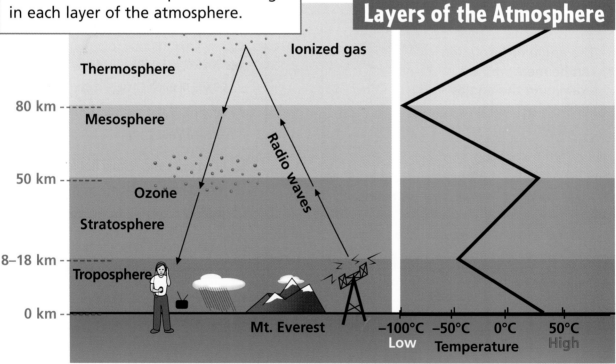

Layers of the Atmosphere

Most weather occurs in the troposphere. The ozone layer in the stratosphere helps shield us from the Sun's ultraviolet light. *Auroras* (the northern and southern lights) may form in the *ionized* (electrically charged) gas in the thermosphere.

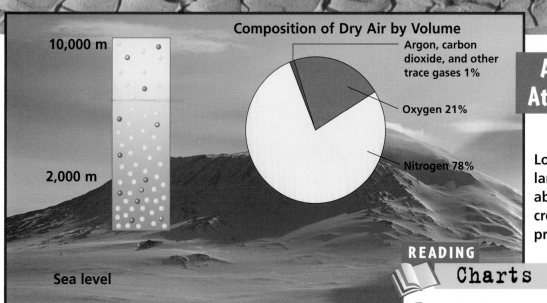

Composition of Dry Air by Volume

10,000 m

2,000 m

Sea level

Argon, carbon dioxide, and other trace gases 1%

Oxygen 21%

Nitrogen 78%

Air in the Atmosphere

Lower altitudes have a larger air column above them, which creates greater air pressure.

READING

Charts

1. What is meant by *trace*?

2. Which gas is the most abundant in the atmosphere?

What Happens to the Air Pressure?

As you go higher in altitude, **air pressure** decreases steadily. Air pressure is the force put on a given area by the weight of the air above it. Air is a mixture of gases. It is made up mostly of *molecules* of nitrogen and oxygen. Molecules are the smallest pieces that a substance can be broken into without changing what the substance is.

The molecules have mass. They are attracted to Earth by gravity, so they have weight.

Normal air pressure is greatest at sea level. There the column of air extending above the surface to the top of the atmosphere is tallest. Sea level air pressure is about 1.04 kilograms per square centimeter (14.7 pounds per square inch). As you go higher in altitude, the height of the air column above you becomes shorter. Therefore the weight of that column—or air pressure—becomes less.

In the lower atmosphere, the composition of air varies very little. Up to an altitude of about 100 km (62 mi), air consists of a mixture of gases, water vapor, and dust particles. Nitrogen and oxygen make up 99 percent of the gases in dry air.

Water vapor is a gas. It should not be confused with clouds or fog, which are made of liquid or solid water. The amount of water vapor in air varies from $\frac{1}{10,000}$ of air in dry arctic regions to $\frac{1}{25}$ of air in moist equatorial regions.

The dust in air is made of particles so tiny that 100,000 lined up would only form a row 1 cm (0.4 in.) long. Some of it comes from Earth's surface, from fires and volcanic eruptions, or from tiny crystals of salt.

▶ **How does air pressure change with altitude?**

What Is Weather?

When you say, "It sure is hot today!" the *it* is the air. You really mean that the air around you is hot. The same is true if you say, "It is windy, " or "It is cloudy," or give any other similar description of the weather . The weather is simply what the lower atmosphere, or troposphere, is like at any given place and time.

The conditions that make up weather are the characteristics that change. They are air temperature, air pressure, amount of moisture in the air, wind, clouds, and rain or snow.

Measuring Temperature

You can measure temperature with a thermometer. Thermometers can use two different temperature scales. The Celsius scale is marked with the letter *C*. The Fahrenheit scale is shown by the letter *F*.

Measuring Air Pressure

Air pressure is measured with a barometer (buh·ROM·i·tuhr). Two common types of barometers are the mercury barometer and the aneroid barometer.

Mercury barometers use a mercury-filled glass tube with one closed end. The open end is submerged in liquid mercury. Air pressure on the mercury pushes it up into the tube. When the weight of the mercury column equals the air pressure, the mercury stops rising.

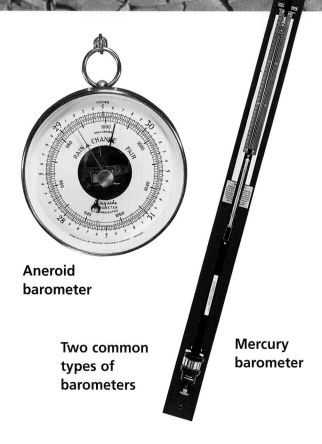

Aneroid barometer

Two common types of barometers

Mercury barometer

An *aneroid* (AN·uh·royd) barometer is an accordion-like metal can with most of the air removed. Inside, a spring balances the outside air pressure. When outside air pressure increases, the can squeezes the spring. When air pressure decreases, the spring pushes outward. A needle inside indicates changes in pressure.

You can monitor and record weather conditions for your own weather station. Measure and record air temperature several times a day. Record daily air pressure by using a barometer or by getting air pressure readings from weather reports.

READING **Main Idea**
What conditions make up weather?

Why It Matters

Have you ever heard a day called a "scorcher"? That means a really hot day. On really hot days, your body can lose a lot of moisture. Your body gives off sweat gradually most of the time. On a hot day, your body tends to give off more and more. That's why it's important to have plenty of drinking water handy on a hot day.

On really cold days, many people have other problems—such as frostbite. You have to cover your face, ears, and hands to avoid contact with air at extremely low temperatures.

e-Journal Visit our Web site **www.science.mmhschool.com** to do a research project on the atmosphere.

Think and Write

1. How do temperatures on Earth depend on angles?

2. List factors that affect temperatures of places on Earth.

3. What is air pressure? How does it change in the atmosphere?

4. What is the troposphere? What happens there?

5. **Critical Thinking** Is the weather one or more than just one thing? Defend your answer.

L·I·N·K·S

MATH LINK

Solve this problem. The sunniest place on Earth is in the eastern Sahara Desert, where sunlight shines an average of 4,300 hours per year. Calculate the percentage of possible sunlight hours a year this number represents. (Assume 12 hours of daylight per day.)

WRITING LINK

Writing a Poem Write a poem about how the weather affects your life. Use words, such as *splash,* that imitate the sound of the weather.

SOCIAL STUDIES LINK

Research the history of the thermometer. The maximum-and-minimum thermometer was invented in 1780 by English scientist James Six. A column of mercury moves up and down a U-shaped tube. An index moves with it, recording the highest and lowest temperatures. Research the history of the thermometer, and write a report for the class.

TECHNOLOGY LINK

LOG ON Visit **www.science.mmhschool.com** for more links.

Water Vapor and Humidity

Get Ready

What if you were walking on this bridge? What would you see and feel all around you? It's fog. What is fog made of? Here's a hint. What if you put a cold glass of lemonade outside on a table on a hot, humid day? What would you see and feel on the outside of the glass?

What is a humid day like? Where is the moisture on a humid day?

Inquiry Skill

You use variables when you identify and separate things in an experiment that can be changed or controlled.

phere as water vapor. Some hit other molecules and return to the liquid. When air is cooled, molecules in the air slow down. The molecules of water vapor in the air also slow down. If they slow enough, water vapor molecules change to molecules of liquid water that collide and stick together to form droplets on cool surfaces. **Condensation** is the changing of a gas into a liquid. You see condensation on shower doors, on cold drink glasses, and as dew on grass in the early morning.

Plants' roots absorb water that has seeped into the ground. Plants transport the liquid water through their roots and stems to their leaves. The leaves then give off water in the process called transpiration. This is the second-largest source of water vapor in the atmosphere.

Two factors determine the amount of humidity in the air. First, there has to be water available to evaporate. Second, the warmer the temperature, the faster the water evaporates. This means that if water is available, warm air will take on more water vapor than cold air.

Relative humidity is a comparison between how much water vapor is in the air and how much the air could hold—at a given temperature.

Relative humidity can affect how a person feels. The higher the relative humidity, the less water can evaporate into the air. The less water, such as sweat, can evaporate from our skin, the warmer and "stickier" we feel.

READING **Main Idea**

How does water get into the air?

QUICK LAB

Transpiration

FOLDABLES™ Make a Two-Column Table. (See p. R 41.) Label as shown.

#3 Communicate	
#5 Predict	

1. Place a clear-plastic bag completely over a houseplant. Tie the bag tightly around the base of the stem. Do not put the soil-filled pot in the bag.

2. **Observe** Place the plant in a sunny location. Observe it several times a day. When you are done, remove the plastic bag from the plant.

3. **Communicate** Use the table to describe what you see inside the bag. Explain what happened.

4. **Draw Conclusions** *Transpiration* sounds like *perspiration*–sweating. How might the two processes be alike?

5. **Predict** How would your results vary if you put the plant in the shade?

What Happens When Warm, Moist Air Cools?

How can warm, moist air cool off? In the lower atmosphere, the air gets colder with increasing altitude.

- Air can cool by being pushed upward over mountains by winds.

- Heating the air also causes it to rise. When the Sun heats the ground, air above the ground warms and rises. As it rises, it expands and cools.

- Air can also be pushed upward when cooler air and warmer air meet. When the two meet, they don't mix. The lighter, warm air is pushed up over the heavier, cold air. As a result, the warm air, pushed higher into the atmosphere, cools.

In each case the end result is the same. As the air rises and cools, the water vapor in it condenses into tiny water droplets, forming clouds.

If the temperature is below the freezing point of water, its water vapor will form a cloud of tiny ice crystals.

In order for water vapor to condense, it must have a surface on which the liquid droplet or ice crystal will form. This surface is provided by tiny dust particles in the air. You will learn more about clouds in the next lesson.

▷ **How can warm air rise and cool?**

How Clouds Form

1 Cloud forms

Warm air

2 Cloud forms

Warm air

3 Cloud forms

Warm air

Cool air

READING

Diagrams

1. What can cause air to rise?

2. What happens to the air temperature as air rises?

L·I·N·K·S

Why It Matters

Have you ever had sweat trickle down your face on a hot day? People sweat every day. Sweating is a way our bodies release wastes. We don't always feel the sweat because we sweat gradually, and it evaporates.

As sweat evaporates, the water droplets absorb heat from the skin's surface, cooling it. In this way your body controls surface temperature.

On very hot days and when you are physically active, you may sweat a lot. The sweat builds up, does not evaporate fast, and collects. On a high-humidity day, you feel even "stickier." On a low-humidity day, the sweat evaporates more quickly.

e-Journal Visit our Web site www.science.mmhschool.com to do a research project on humidity.

Think and Write

1. Where does water vapor in the air come from? What process produces it?

2. How is relative humidity different from humidity?

3. What causes water vapor to change into droplets of liquid water?

4. How does water vapor get cooled in the atmosphere?

5. **Critical Thinking** Would you say that the Sun is a cause of clouds? Defend your answer.

WRITING LINK

Personal Narrative Why are you less comfortable in higher relative humidity? Write about a day in your life when higher relative humidity affected you.

MATH LINK

Find the heat index. Use an almanac to find a heat index prepared by the weather service. This chart tells how warm a person feels at a particular temperature and humidity level. Using the chart, find the heat index for each of the days in the table below. Then use newspaper weather reports for one week last summer. Find the heat index for each of those days.

	Mon	Tues	Wed	Thurs	Fri
High temp.	25°C	35°C	30°C	35°C	25°C
Relative humidity	90%	97%	89%	48%	45%

ART LINK

Make a poster. Very hot, humid weather can be dangerous. Make a poster warning about the dangers of very hot, humid weather. Include a list of safety tips.

TECHNOLOGY LINK

 LOG ON Visit www.science.mmhschool.com for more links.

Clouds and Precipitation

Vocabulary

stratus cloud, D44

cumulus cloud, D44

cirrus cloud, D44

fog, D44

precipitation, D46

Get Ready

How can you predict the weather without using the instruments weather forecasters use? Look at the sky. There are clues up there. They're called clouds. Different kinds of clouds bring different kinds of weather. What is a cloud? What makes a cloud form? What do evaporation and condensation have to do with it?

Inquiry Skill

You infer when you form an idea from facts or observations.

Explore Activity

How Do Clouds Form?

Materials

hot tap water

2 identical clear containers

mug

3 ice cubes

Procedure

BE CAREFUL! Be careful handling the hot water.

1. Chill container 1 by putting it in a refrigerator or on ice for about ten minutes.

2. Fill a mug with hot water.

3. **Make a Model** Fill container 2 with the hot water. Place empty cold container 1 upside down on top of container 2 with the water. Fit the mouths together carefully. Place the ice cubes on top of container 1.

4. **Observe** Record your observations.

Drawing Conclusions

1. **Communicate** What did you observe?

2. **Communicate** Where did this take place?

3. **Infer** Where did the water come from? Explain what made it happen.

4. **FURTHER INQUIRY** **Infer** Do clouds form better in dry or moist air? Conduct an experiment to test your inference. What materials will you need? What will you do?

Main Idea Water vapor and ice form clouds that produce precipitation.

How Do Clouds Form?

What has to happen for a cloud to form? Clouds are made up of tiny water droplets or ice crystals. The air is filled with water vapor. When the air is cooled, the water vapor condenses. That is, the water molecules clump together around dust and other particles in the air. They form droplets of water.

Clouds look different depending on what they are made of. Water-droplet clouds tend to have sharp, well-defined edges. If the cloud is very thick, it may look gray, or even black. That's because sunlight is unable to pass through. Ice-crystal clouds tend to have fuzzy, less distinct edges. They also look whiter.

All clouds form in the troposphere. There are three basic cloud forms. **Stratus clouds** form in blanketlike layers. **Cumulus clouds** are puffy clouds that appear to rise up from a flat bottom. **Cirrus clouds** form at very high altitudes out of ice crystals and have a wispy, featherlike shape. If rain or snow falls from a cloud, the term *nimbo* or *nimbus*—for "rain"—is added to the cloud's name.

Clouds are further grouped into families by height and form. There are low clouds, middle clouds, high clouds, and clouds that develop upward— clouds of vertical development. Cumulonimbus clouds develop upward. These clouds bring thunderstorms.

Stratus clouds

Cumulus clouds

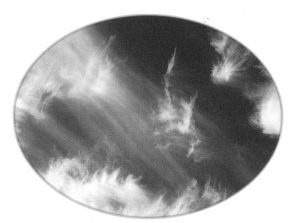
Cirrus clouds

They can start as low clouds and reach up to the highest clouds. If moist air at ground level cools, a cloud can form right there. A cloud at ground level is called **fog**.

▶ **What are three basic cloud forms?**

Types of Clouds

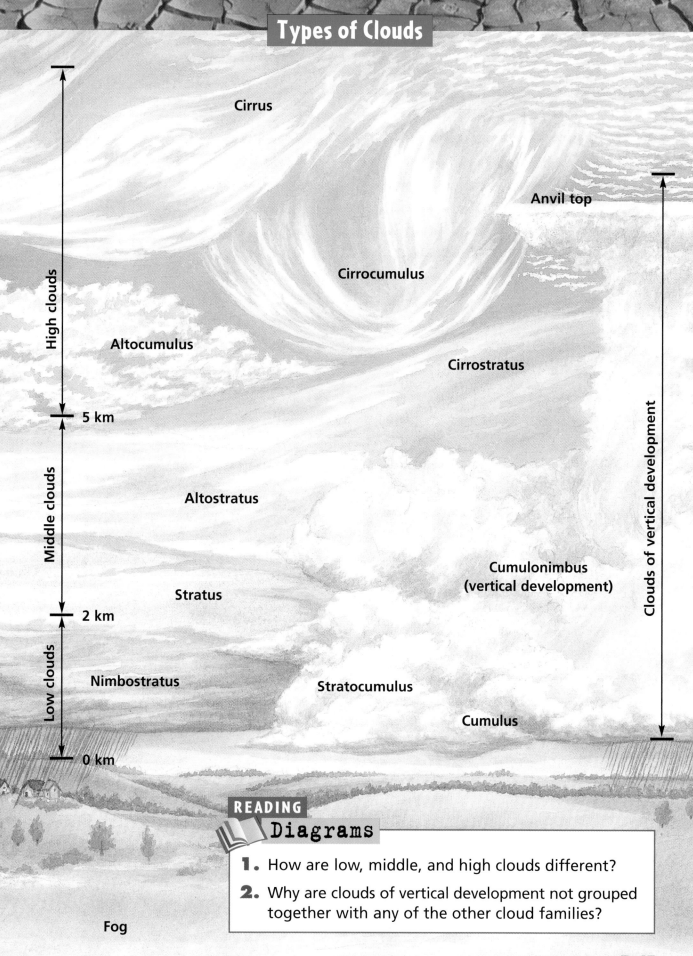

Cirrus

Anvil top

Cirrocumulus

High clouds

Altocumulus

Cirrostratus

5 km

Middle clouds

Altostratus

Clouds of vertical development

Cumulonimbus (vertical development)

Stratus

2 km

Low clouds

Nimbostratus

Stratocumulus

Cumulus

0 km

Fog

READING
Diagrams

1. How are low, middle, and high clouds different?

2. Why are clouds of vertical development not grouped together with any of the other cloud families?

What Is Precipitation?

How do rain and snow form and fall? **Precipitation** is any form of water particles that falls from the atmosphere and reaches the ground. Precipitation can be liquid (rain) or solid (such as snow).

Clouds are made up of tiny water droplets or ice crystals—only about $\frac{1}{50}$ of a millimeter across. These tiny particles are so light that they remain "hanging" in the air. This is why many clouds do not form precipitation.

Precipitation occurs when cloud droplets or ice crystals join together and become heavy enough to fall. They clump around particles of dust in the air. Each particle is like a *nucleus* that the water molecules condense around. The chart shows the different types of precipitation and how they form.

▷ **When does precipitation occur?**

READING
Diagrams

1. Classify the types of precipitation into two groups—solids and liquids.

2. Which types of precipitation form in similar ways?

Types of Precipitation

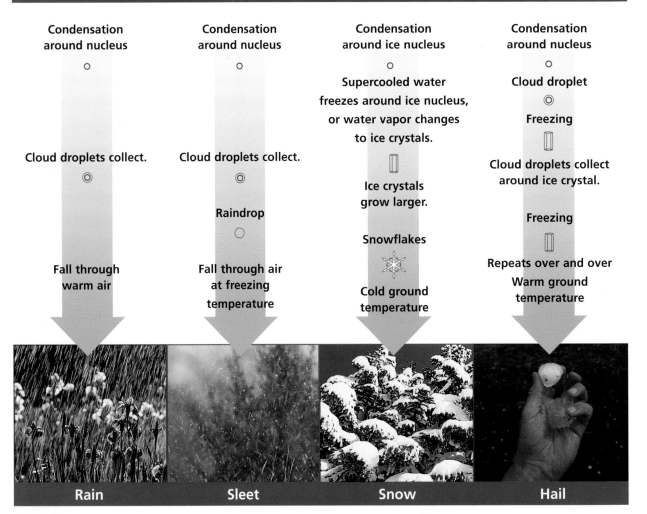

Condensation around nucleus	Condensation around nucleus	Condensation around ice nucleus	Condensation around nucleus
○	○	○	○
		Supercooled water freezes around ice nucleus, or water vapor changes to ice crystals.	Cloud droplet
			Freezing
Cloud droplets collect.	Cloud droplets collect.	Ice crystals grow larger.	Cloud droplets collect around ice crystal.
◎	◎		Freezing
	Raindrop	Snowflakes	
	○		Repeats over and over
Fall through warm air	Fall through air at freezing temperature	Cold ground temperature	Warm ground temperature
Rain	**Sleet**	**Snow**	**Hail**

Are Cloud Type and Precipitation Related?

Do certain kinds of clouds give certain kinds of precipitation? Yes.

- In tall clouds there is more chance for droplets to run into one another and combine, making larger raindrops.

- Precipitation from large cumulus clouds is often heavy rain or snow showers that don't last too long.

- Precipitation from stratus clouds is usually long lasting, with smaller drops of rain or snowflakes.

- Clouds with great vertical development hold a lot of water. These clouds are very *turbulent*, or violent. Their tops often reach heights where it is below freezing. They often produce great downpours. They also sometimes produce *hail*. Hail is pellets or lumps of ice.

These clouds have updrafts—strong winds that move up inside. Hail forms when updrafts in these huge clouds hurl ice pellets upward again and again. As the pellets fall, they become coated with water. As they rise, the water freezes into an icy outer shell. This process usually happens over and over, adding more and more layers to the hailstones. The more violent the updrafts, the bigger the hailstones can get before they fall to the ground.

READING Main Idea
What kind of cloud can produce hail? Why?

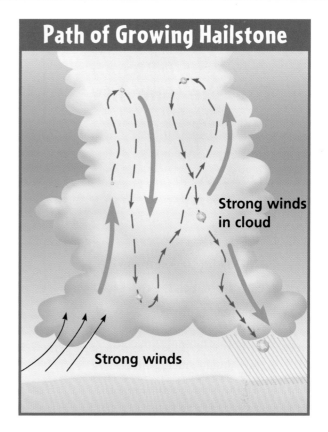

Path of Growing Hailstone

Strong winds in cloud

Strong winds

Hailstones form in layers and can sometimes grow very large. Hailstorms can be very dangerous.

QUICK LAB

Feel the Humidity

FOLDABLES Make an Eight-Row Chart. (See p. R 44.) Label as shown.

Time		Humid Day	Dry Day
1 min.	30 s		
	30 s		
2 min.	30 s		
	30 s		
3 min.	30 s		
	30 s		
#5 Infer			

1. **Observe** Use a thermometer to determine the air temperature. Use the chart to record the air temperature.

2. Put the thermometer in cold water. Slowly add warm water until the water temperature matches the air temperature.

3. Wrap a 5-cm-square piece of old cotton cloth around the bulb of the thermometer. Gently hold it with a rubber band. Dampen the cloth in the water.

4. **Observe** Gently wave the thermometer in the air. Note the temperatures every 30 seconds for 3 minutes. Record them on your chart.

5. **Infer** What happened to the temperature of the wet cloth? How does the cloth feel? Explain on the bottom of your chart.

6. **Infer** If you try this experiment on a day that is humid and on a day that is dry will you get the same results?

How Do You Record How Cloudy It Is?

As you observe the weather each day, you might wish to record the types of clouds you see in the sky. You can use the charts in this lesson to indicate the cloud family and the types of clouds.

Try to estimate the cloud cover—that is, the amount of the sky covered by clouds. Use the terms *clear, scattered clouds, partly cloudy, mostly cloudy,* or *overcast* to describe cloud cover.

One way to record cloud cover is to make a weather station model. Start by drawing a circle for each day. An empty circle means "clear skies." A fully shaded circle means "completely overcast." Portions of a circle are shaded to show different amounts of cloud cover.

Precipitation is measured with a rain gauge. You can make a simple rain gauge from an empty coffee can. Place it outside, open end up, away from buildings or trees. When the precipitation stops, measure its depth in the can. Keep track of the type of precipitation and how much falls.

▷ **What are the terms used to record cloud cover?**

○	Clear
●	Overcast
◔	Scattered clouds
◑	Partly cloudy
◕	Mostly cloudy

Symbols are used to show cloud cover on a weather station model.

Why It Matters

If you ever had a baseball game rained out, you know how rain can ruin your day.

Rain may ruin your plans for a day, and flooding can sometimes cause disasters. However, rain is vital for life on Earth. Rain helps crops grow. Rain helps build the amount of water in wells and water-collecting areas, such as reservoirs. If you ever had a drought in your area, a time when there is little or no precipitation, you know how scarce water can be.

e-Journal Visit our Web site www.science.mmhschool.com to do a research project on clouds.

Think and Write

1. How do clouds form?

2. What are some different types of precipitation? Why are there different types?

3. Explain the difference between the way hail forms and the way sleet forms.

4. How can you measure and describe the amount of precipitation and cloud cover on a given day?

5. **Critical Thinking** "Sun showers" are sudden rainfalls on a sunny day. How can a sun shower happen?

L·I·N·K·S

LITERATURE LINK

Read *The Great Johnstown Flood,* the story of the storm that destroyed a town. When you finish reading, think about how you would prepare for a flood. Try the activities at the end of the book.

The Great Johnstown Flood

by Lisa Norby

MATH LINK

Calculate accuracy. Observe clouds in your area each day for a week. Predict weather based on precipitation those clouds are likely to produce. Record how accurate your predictions are. Then, calculate your accuracy in percent.

WRITING LINK

Writing a Story The Inuit have more than 20 different words for snow. Why do you think this is so? Write a "how" or "why" story about why the Inuit have so many words for snow.

TECHNOLOGY LINK

Science Newsroom CD-ROM Choose *On the Vapor Trail* to learn more about how warm, moist air reacts when it cools.

LOG ON Visit www.science.mmhschool.com for more links.

Flood: Good News or Bad?

Can you imagine a flood being good news? It was to many ancient Egyptians living near the Nile River. They looked forward to its annual summer flood. Land that was flooded was better for crops!

No one knew for sure why the flood came. Some people believed that great rains fell near the source of the Nile to start the flood. Much of the water actually comes from rains that fall in the mountains of Ethiopia.

Ethiopia has many mountains over 4,000 meters (13,000 feet) tall. In June the monsoons blow from the South Atlantic over the rain forests of Africa. When the winds reach the mountains of Ethiopia, giant rain clouds let loose their water in great thunderstorms. Rain-filled mountain streams join to form a great river. The river carries the water to the Nile. By July the water reaches Egypt and produces the flood.

Summer winds

MEDITERRANEAN SEA

EGYPT

SAUDI ARABIA

NILE RIVER

RED SEA

SUDAN

ETHIOPIA

and Society

Aswan Dam, Egypt

Today the flood waters are stopped soon after they reach Egypt. A high dam holds back the water to form a great lake. The good news is that buildings on the shore are no longer swept away. Farmers no longer depend on floods to plant one crop each year. Now they have water to plant during summer and winter.

Stopping the flood has changed the environment, and that's bad news. The flood kept the fields fertile; but now farmers must use fertilizer. The Mediterranean Sea was nourished by mud from the Nile. Now fish that were common are gone, and a serious disease is spread by snails thriving in the Nile's slow waters.

What Did I Learn?

1. Where did the Nile flooding start?

   A in the Red Sea
   B in the Mediterranean Sea
   C in the mountains of Ethiopia
   D in Saudi Arabia

2. Stopping the Nile flooding

   F kept the fields fertile.
   G increased the fish population.
   H killed off the snails.
   J changed the environment.

LOG ON Visit www.science.mmhschool.com to learn more about floods.

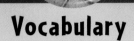
Air Pressure and Wind

Vocabulary

wind, D55

convection cell, D55

sea breeze, D56

land breeze, D56

Coriolis effect, D57

isobar, D59

Get Ready

What makes the air move? What causes wind? Winds make these kites fly. Some winds move so fast and powerfully, they can knock down trees or even lift trucks into the air. Some winds can be so gentle, they hardly ruffle your hair. Air moves from one place to another because of differences in air pressure. What causes these differences?

Inquiry Skill

You **use variables** when you identify and separate things in an experiment that can be changed or controlled.

Explore Activity

What Can Change Air Pressure?

Materials

plastic jar with hole in bottom

plastic sandwich bag

rubber band

masking tape

Procedure

1 **Make a Model** Set up a bag-and-jar system as shown. Make sure the masking tape covers the hole in the jar. Have a partner place both hands on the jar and hold it firmly. Reach in and slowly pull up on the bottom of the bag. Describe what happens.

2 **Experiment** Pull the small piece of tape off the hole in the bottom of the jar. Repeat step 1. Push in on the bag. Record your results.

3 **Observe** Place some small bits of paper on the table. Hold the jar close to the table. Point the hole toward the bits of paper. Pull up on the bag, and observe and record what happens.

4 **Experiment** Do just the opposite. Push the bag back into the jar. What happened?

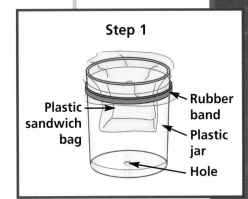

Step 1

Plastic sandwich bag

Rubber band

Plastic jar

Hole

Drawing Conclusions

1 **Observe** What differences did you observe with the hole taped and with the tape removed?

2 **Infer** Explain what happened each time you pushed the bag back into the jar. How does this model show air pressure changes?

3 **FURTHER INQUIRY** **Use Variables** What happens to the amount of space air takes up if it is warmed? Use the model to test your hypothesis.

Main Idea Differences in air pressure on Earth's surface cause wind.

How Can Air Pressure Change?

Many factors affect the pressure.

Volume

Pulling up on the bag in the diagram below increases the volume inside the bag-jar system. The amount of air inside stays the same. The air inside the jar spreads out into the larger volume. The air pressure inside the bag-jar becomes less. The outside air pushes in harder than the inside air pushes out. That extra force pushing in is what you pull against as you pull up on the bag.

Height Above Earth's Surface

Air pressure depends on the weight of its molecules pressing down on a given area. Molecules are closer together, or more dense, at sea level than high in the atmosphere. Denser air weighs more than an equal volume of less dense air and pushes down harder. That is why air pressure is higher at sea level than high in the atmosphere.

Temperature

Air pressure also depends on temperature. When air is heated, its molecules speed up and spread out into a larger space. The same volume of air weighs less, and the pressure decreases.

Amount of Water Vapor

Air is a mixture of nitrogen, oxygen, and other gases. Adding water vapor to air also affects air pressure. Water vapor molecules weigh less than oxygen or nitrogen molecules. Moist air exerts less pressure than dry air.

READING Diagrams

Explain what happens to the air pressure inside the jar as you push down on the bag.

> How would an increase in temperature affect air pressure?

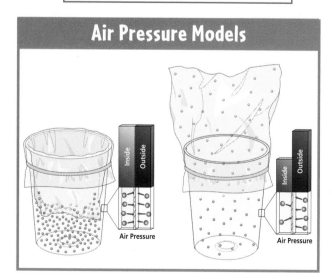

Air Pressure Models

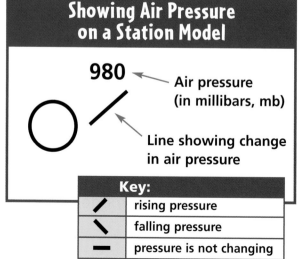

Showing Air Pressure on a Station Model

980 — Air pressure (in millibars, mb)

Line showing change in air pressure

Key:	
/	rising pressure
\	falling pressure
—	pressure is not changing

Why Do Winds Blow?

Think of what happens if you put a blob of soft clay on a table and push down on it, using a flat hand. The clay squishes out from under your fingers, where the pressure is high. It moves to the spaces between your fingers, where the pressure is lower.

Air acts in a similar way. Denser air exerts a higher pressure than less dense air. Like the clay, denser air flows toward less dense air. This flow of air is wind. Air that moves horizontally is called **wind**. Air that rises is an *updraft*. Air that sinks is a *downdraft*.

Convection Cells

How can air become more or less dense? As the Sun's rays hit an area, they transfer energy to the air. The air heats up. Because it is warmer, the heated air is less dense. Then, just like a cork in water, the warm air rises above the surrounding cooler, denser air. On the other hand, if a region of air is cooled, it becomes denser and sinks.

This unequal heating and cooling of the air often makes a pattern of rising air, sinking air, and winds, called a **convection** (kuhn·VEK·shuhn) **cell**. A convection cell is a part of the atmosphere where air moves in a circular pattern because of unequal heating and cooling.

The drawing shows how a convection cell forms. Cities A and B have the same air pressure. Then direct sunlight heats city A. The air above it warms and expands. It becomes less dense and rises, forming an updraft. The air pressure goes down. The unheated air on either side has a higher pressure. This air moves in toward the low-pressure area, making a surface wind.

▷ **How are winds produced?**

READING Diagrams

Use the diagram to explain what happens to city B during the formation of the convection cell.

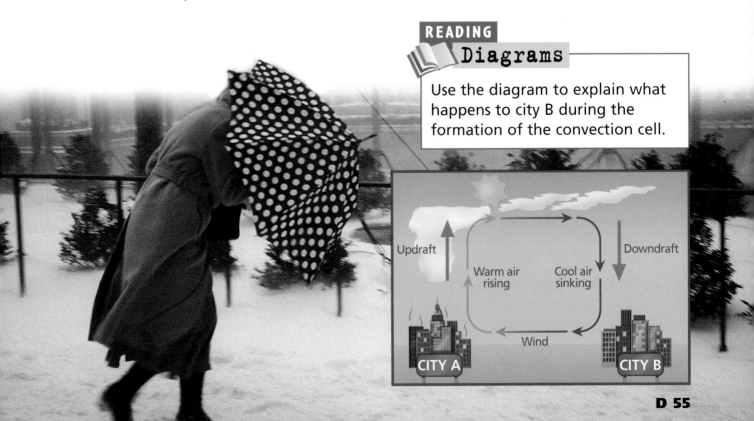

Updraft
Downdraft
Warm air rising
Cool air sinking
Wind
CITY A
CITY B

Warm air

Cold air

Sea breeze

Warm air

Cold air

Valley breeze

What Are Sea and Land Breezes?

An example of convection is a breeze that occurs along a coastline. Land warms faster than water. On sunny days air over land warms faster than air next to it over the sea. The warm air expands and rises. Cooler air from over the ocean replaces the rising warm air. A wind blows onto the land. A wind that blows from the sea toward the land is called a **sea breeze**.

At night the reverse happens. The air over the land cools more rapidly than the air over the water. A **land breeze** blows from land toward the water.

Convection cells also occur along mountains. As the Sun shines on a mountain during the day, the slope heats up faster than the valley below. Air over the slope warms and rises.

READING

Diagrams

These pictures show what happens during the day. How would you show what happens at night?

Cooler air over the valley replaces the rising warm air, creating a *valley breeze* that blows up the slope. At night the mountain slope cools rapidly. This causes a *mountain breeze* to blow down the slope.

▷ **How are sea and land breezes produced?**

What Is the Coriolis Effect?

Earth's rotation affects winds blowing across its surface. As Earth rotates, every spot on its surface moves with it. However, in the same 24-hour period, places near the poles travel a shorter distance than places near the equator. This means that places near the poles are moving slower!

Now what if you are in an airplane flying in a straight line from the North Pole to Chicago? While you are in the air, Earth is *rotating*, or spinning, underneath you. Earth rotates counterclockwise as seen from the North Pole. As Earth rotates, Chicago is moving west to east. To someone in Chicago, though, the plane's flight path seems to curve to the southwest.

The same thing happens with winds blowing from the North Pole. Because Earth rotates, the winds seem to curve to the right as they head southward.

No matter which way the wind blows, it will curve to the right in the Northern Hemisphere. This curving is known as the **Coriolis effect**. In the Southern Hemisphere, the Coriolis effect causes winds to curve to the left. This is because, as viewed from the South Pole, Earth rotates clockwise. The effect works on other moving objects as well, such as missiles and rockets.

▷ **What causes the Coriolis effect?**

Coriolis Effect

If you were standing at the North Pole looking south, this arrow would appear to curve to the right.

Rotation

If you were standing at the South Pole looking north, this arrow would appear to curve to the left.

How Are Global Wind Patterns Produced?

Year round the equator is heated strongly by sunlight. The air becomes very warm. Heat also causes evaporation, so the air becomes moist. Warm, moist air over the equator creates a zone of low pressure around the globe.

As the air at the equator warms, it becomes less dense and rises. It rises to the top of the troposphere and spreads out, moving north and south. As the air moves away from the equator, it cools and becomes denser. At about 30° north and south latitudes, the cold air begins to sink toward the surface. This sinking air creates a high-pressure zone on both sides of the equator at these latitudes. A belt of winds is set in motion around Earth by air moving from these high-pressure zones toward the low pressure at the equator. These are the *trade winds*. The Coriolis effect curves these winds, as you see in the diagram.

The poles get very low-angle sunlight, and the air there is very cold. Cold, dense air can hold very little water vapor. Cold, dry air over the poles has high pressure. Air at the poles moves toward 60° latitude, forming winds. Because of the Coriolis effect, the winds curve. These are the polar *easterly winds*. *Easterly* means the wind blows "from the east."

Other winds occur between 60° latitude and the poles as well as between 30° and 60° latitudes. Between 30° and 60° latitudes is the zone of *westerly winds*. The continental United States is in the zone of westerly winds.

▶ **What causes the global trade winds?**

Global Wind Zones

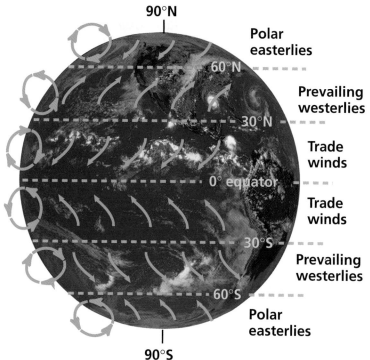

90°N

Polar easterlies

60°N

Prevailing westerlies

30°N

Trade winds

0° equator

Trade winds

30°S

Prevailing westerlies

60°S

Polar easterlies

90°S

READING

Diagrams

Make a table listing different global wind zones and a description of the directions in which winds move in each zone.

N
W ← → E
S

What Are Isobars?

Why is it important to know about air pressure? Knowing where the air pressure is high or low allows you to predict which way air will move. This is why weather scientists make maps showing air pressure. They start by plotting the air pressure at many different locations on a map. Then they connect all places with the same air pressure with a line. A line on a map connecting places with equal air pressure is called an **isobar**. Isobars make pressure patterns easier to see.

Find the series of circular isobars in the west, surrounding a region of high pressure (H). This pattern is called a *high-pressure system*. Since the center has higher pressure than its surroundings, winds blow outward from the center in a clockwise pattern.

A similar set of isobars in the east marks a *low-pressure system* (L). In a low-pressure system, the central region is surrounded by higher pressure. The winds blow in toward the center in a counterclockwise pattern.

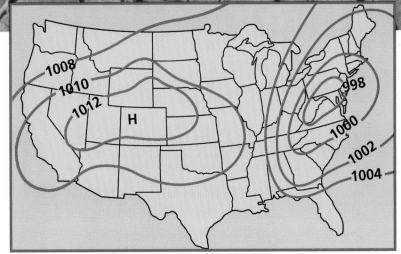

The pressure on each isobar is in millibars (mb).

Isobars also help scientists predict how fast air will move. Big differences in air pressure over short distances cause strong winds. This is shown on a map by drawing closely spaced isobars. Small differences in air pressure cause gentle winds. This is shown by widely spaced isobars.

You show wind on a station model with a straight line touching the circle. The line tells where the wind is blowing from. "Feathers" are used to show speed.

READING Main Idea

How do isobars help scientists predict how air will move?

How Winds Blow

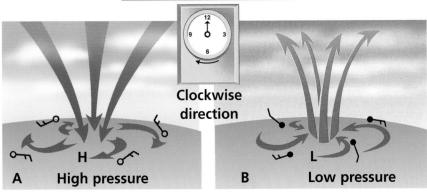

Clockwise direction

A High pressure

B Low pressure

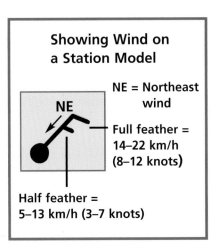

Showing Wind on a Station Model

NE

NE = Northeast wind

Full feather = 14–22 km/h (8–12 knots)

Half feather = 5–13 km/h (3–7 knots)

A Weather Station Model

A weather station model includes temperature, cloud cover, air pressure, pressure tendency, wind speed, and wind direction. The circle is at the location of the station. You will interpret the data, using the information from the weather station models to answer questions and solve problems.

Wind direction (from north)

Wind speed (knots or km/h)

Air temperature (°C) (It may also be recorded in °F.) → 13 | 1014

Air pressure (mb)

Pressure change

Cloud cover

34 ◯ 1004
Dallas

28 ◑ 980
Charlotte

14 ◔ 1012
Oakland

30 ◑ 996
Tampa

Procedure

1 **Use Numbers** Look carefully at the Dallas weather station model. How fast is the wind blowing? What is the wind direction? Record your answers.

2 **Interpret Data** What other information does this weather station model give you?

3 Look at the other weather station models. Make a table recording weather conditions for each city.

Drawing Conclusions

1 Compare the information in the table you made with these station models. Which way is the information easier to interpret?

2 **Interpret Data** Where was wind fastest? Slowest? Which tells you this information more quickly, the table or the models?

3 **Communicate** Compare and contrast other weather conditions in the cities.

Why It Matters

Wind can be very useful. It is often used as a source of power. Wind turns windmills, special machines that produce electricity. They run the machinery that grinds grain. Windmills are also used to pump water.

Wind carries pollen to flowers. Seeds form as a result. Many kinds of seeds, in turn, are carried by wind to new places.

e-Journal Visit our Web site **www.science.mmhschool.com** to do a research project on wind.

Think and Write

1. What makes air pressure change?

2. What causes wind to blow in a particular direction?

3. Why are there zones of winds around the world?

4. Interpret Data On a weather map, how can you compare the speed and direction of winds in different locations?

5. Critical Thinking How might temperatures near the ocean compare with those inland in winter? In summer? Explain.

L·I·N·K·S

LITERATURE LINK

Read *The Sky-Watchers*, the story of how two students maintained a weather station. When you finish reading, think about how you would build a weather station. Try the activities at the end of the book.

THE SKY-WATCHERS

by Patricia Baehr
Illustrated by Eldon Doty

WRITING LINK

Expository Writing Research and write a report on the Beaufort Wind Scale. Include its history. Draw a conclusion about its importance.

MATH LINK

Calculate weather factors. Collect a week's worth of national weather maps from a newspaper. Select a region of the country, such as the Midwest or Southeast. Calculate its average temperature, wind speed, and air pressure.

SOCIAL STUDIES LINK

Write a report. Research the origin of the term "trade winds," and write a report on your findings.

TECHNOLOGY LINK

 LOG ON Visit **www.science.mmhschool.com** for more links.

Weather: It's Instrumental!

You turn on the TV to catch the weather forecast. The satellite image looks cool, but all you want to know is how warm it is, whether it's windy, and if you're going to get wet on your way to school. Where does that information come from? Not from space, but from a set of instruments at a nearby weather station.

To find the temperature, you need a thermometer. To find how much rain has fallen, you need a rain gauge. Put a straight-sided bucket outside to collect rain water. Later, stick a ruler in the bucket to measure how much rain fell.

Wonder how much moisture is in the air? Your hair is a good indicator! It gets frizzier when it's raining or very humid outside. That's because hair lengthens (and kinks up) when the air is moist. Forecasters use "hair hygrometers" to measure humidity. Hygrometers have pens that are attached to human or horse hairs. As the hair changes length, the pen graphs the change in humidity.

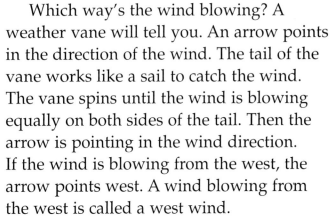

Which way's the wind blowing? A weather vane will tell you. An arrow points in the direction of the wind. The tail of the vane works like a sail to catch the wind. The vane spins until the wind is blowing equally on both sides of the tail. Then the arrow is pointing in the wind direction. If the wind is blowing from the west, the arrow points west. A wind blowing from the west is called a west wind.

How windy is it? The speed of the wind is measured with an anemometer. It uses a set of cups attached to a central pole. As the cups catch the wind, they spin around like a pinwheel. The faster the wind, the faster they spin. Now you can set up a weather station right in your own backyard!

Write About It

1. What weather information do you need before you go outside? What instruments help get that information?

2. What would it take to set up a weather station in your neighborhood or outside your window?

LOG ON Visit www.science.mmhschool.com to learn more about measuring weather.

Chapter 10 Review

Vocabulary

Fill each blank with the best word or words from the list.

> **barometer,** D34
> **cirrus cloud,** D44
> **condensation,** D39
> **Coriolis effect,** D57
> **evaporation,** D38
> **humidity,** D38
> **land breeze,** D56
> **precipitation,** D46
> **sea breeze,** D56
> **stratus cloud,** D44

1. Rain, snow, and sleet are kinds of _____.

2. The _____ causes winds to follow a curved path over Earth's surface.

3. A(n) _____ forms in blanketlike layers.

4. Liquid changes directly to a gas by the process called _____.

5. The amount of water vapor in the air is called _____.

6. Wind blowing from the ocean toward the land is called a(n) _____.

7. Wind blowing from the land toward the ocean is called a(n) _____.

8. The process that turns water vapor into raindrops is called _____.

9. A high, wispy cloud made of ice crystals is a(n) _____.

10. A(n) _____ measures air pressure.

Test Prep

11. In a low-presure system _____.
- **A** winds blow out
- **B** winds blow clockwise
- **C** winds blow west
- **D** winds blow inward, counterclockwise

12. Weather takes place in the _____.
- **F** thermosphere
- **G** mesosphere
- **H** troposphere
- **J** stratosphere

13. Water drops that collect on a cold glass of lemonade come from _____.
- **A** the lemonade
- **B** the air
- **C** a puddle
- **D** the glass itself

14. Isobars indicate _____.
- **F** humidity
- **G** temperature
- **H** air pressure
- **J** cloud cover

15. On a hot day, a lake is likely to be _____.

   A cooler than nearby land

   B hotter than nearby land

   C the same temperature as the land

   D the cause of the heat

Concepts and Skills

16. Reading in Science Write a paragraph explaining why north winds blow to the southwest.

17. Safety Why do you need to be careful on hot days when the relative humidity is high? Write a paragraph explaining your answer.

18. Scientific Methods How much does humidity change over a day? Write a design for an experiment that would test this.

19. INQUIRY SKILL Interpret Data You are given this information on a weather map: What kind of weather is city A having? What kind of weather is city B having? Write a paragraph explaining your answer.

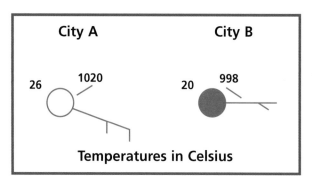

Temperatures in Celsius

20. Critical Thinking What if there were no plants? Do you think Earth would still get as much rain as it does now? Write your ideas. Describe how you might test them.

Did You Ever Wonder?

INQUIRY SKILL **Infer** You look up in the sky and see clouds. Why don't those clouds fall to the ground?

LOG ON Visit www.science.mmhschool.com to boost your test scores.

Weather Patterns and Climate

Did You Ever Wonder?

Why is a desert hot and dry? Conditions in the Mojave Desert
in California are partly caused by the mountains you see in the
background. Rain falls on the other side of the mountains before
it can reach the Mojave. Why does one side of a mountain get a lot
of rain while the other side gets very little?

INQUIRY SKILL Infer Deserts are hot during the day. How can they get so
cool at night?

Air Masses and Fronts

Get Ready

Have you ever watched a "wall" of clouds heading toward you? Did the clouds bring gentle, steady rain or heavy downpours? Knowing what kind of weather is on the way can help you make plans.

Part of what weather forecasters need to watch for is approaching air masses and fronts. Why might your weather today depend on what someone else's weather was like yesterday?

Inquiry Skill

You interpret data **when you use the information that has been gathered to answer questions or solve a problem.**

Explore Activity

How Can You Compare Weather?

Materials

station model key

newspaper weather map (optional)

pencil

crayons

Procedure

Communicate Think of the country in large regions—the Northeast, the Southwest, and the coasts. Write a report for the weather in each region based on the map you see here.

Drawing Conclusions

1 Infer Which areas are having warm, rainy weather?

2 Infer Where is the weather cool and dry?

3 Predict How do you think weather in any part of the country may change, based on the data in this map? Give reasons for your answer. How would you check your predictions?

4 FURTHER INQUIRY Interpret Data What will tomorrow's weather be like? Interpret the information on the weather map in the morning paper. Compare your interpretation to the actual weather during the day.

W   E

Lines are drawn to show wind direction, not speed. This is a wind coming from the east, going west—an east wind.

San Francisco

Temperatures here are given in degrees Fahrenheit.

® = rain

Main Idea Weather changes often occur at fronts, where different air masses meet.

How Do Air Masses Affect Weather?

Weather maps show that cities across a large region can share the same weather. They also show how the weather in different areas can differ.

Why are weather conditions in one part of a country different from those in another part? Look back at the map on page D69. Some of the cities are having clear, cool weather. The air throughout this region is cool and dry. Other cities are having warmer, cloudy weather. The air throughout this region is warm and moist. A large region of the atmosphere where the air has similar properties throughout is called an **air mass**.

An air mass gets its properties from the region where it forms. Air over the Gulf of Mexico is above very warm water. The water warms the air, and evaporation from the Gulf adds water vapor. The air becomes warm and moist. Air masses are named for the region they come from.

As air masses move, they bring these conditions with them. What happens if a cool, moist air mass moves over an area that has warm, dry weather? The warm, dry weather will change.

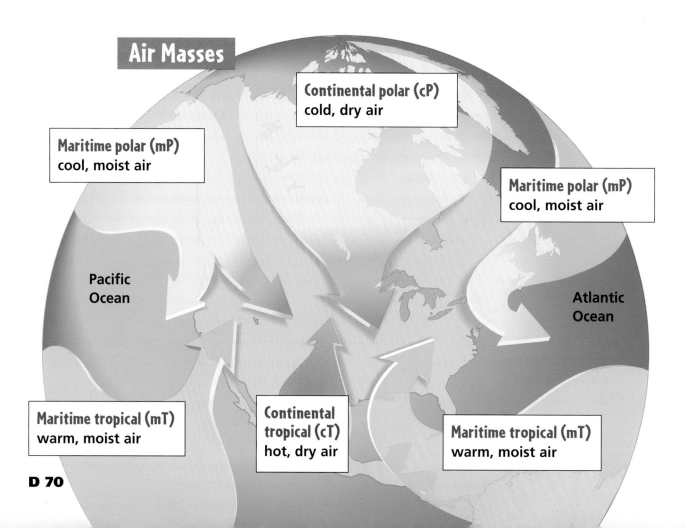

Air Masses

Continental polar (cP)
cold, dry air

Maritime polar (mP)
cool, moist air

Maritime polar (mP)
cool, moist air

Pacific Ocean

Atlantic Ocean

Maritime tropical (mT)
warm, moist air

Continental tropical (cT)
hot, dry air

Maritime tropical (mT)
warm, moist air

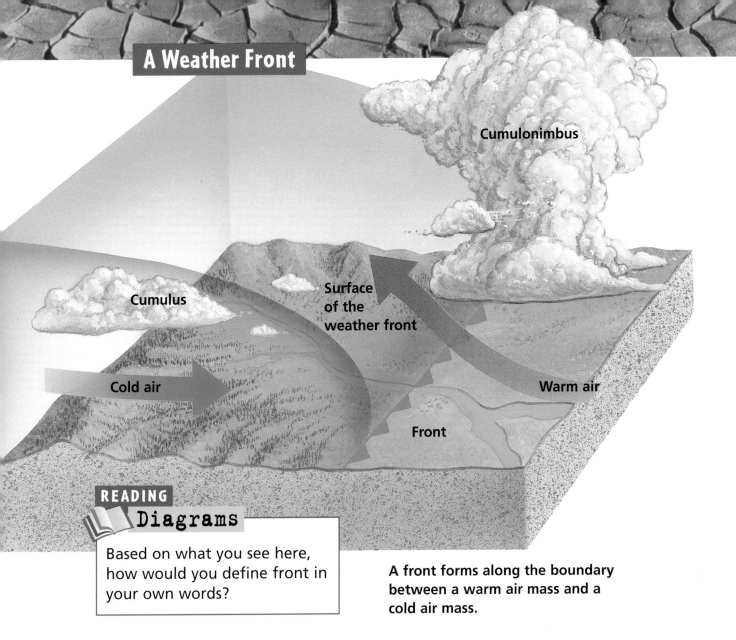

A Weather Front

Cumulonimbus

Cumulus

Surface of the weather front

Cold air

Warm air

Front

READING

Diagrams

Based on what you see here, how would you define front in your own words?

A front forms along the boundary between a warm air mass and a cold air mass.

Once an air mass is formed, it is moved by global winds. In the United States, global winds tend to move air masses from west to east.

Air masses with different conditions can "meet." That is, one runs into another. What happens when air masses with different temperatures meet? They don't mix together. Instead, a narrow boundary forms between them. This boundary is called a **front**. It marks the leading edge, or front, of an air mass that is moving into an area where another air mass is moving out. Weather changes rapidly at fronts. That's because you pass from one kind of air mass into another. Fronts often cause rainy, unsettled weather.

READING **Sequence of Events**

What happens when a cold air mass meets with a warm air mass?

QUICK LAB

Weather Prediction

FOLDABLES™ Make a Four-Door Book. (See p. R 44.) Label the tabs as shown.

1. Find a weather map in a newspaper that shows the weather across the United States. Be sure the map shows at least one cold front or warm front in the western part of the country. Look at your map. Use the book to describe the weather in your state.

2. Use your book to describe the weather in each region of the country–northwest, southwest, southeast, northeast.

3. **Infer** Weather patterns move from west to east across the United States. How do you think the weather just east of the front will change in the next day or so? Explain under the tabs of your Four-Door Book.

▷ **What kind of weather does a cold front usually produce?**

How Do Fronts Affect Weather?

- In a **cold front**, cold air moves in under a warm air mass. Cold fronts often bring brief, heavy storms. There may be thunderstorms and strong winds. After the storm the skies are usually clearer, and the weather is usually cooler and drier.

- In a **warm front**, warm air moves in over a cold air mass. Warm fronts often bring light, steady rain or snow. The precipitation may last for days. Winds are usually light. Warm fronts may also bring fog—stratus clouds that form near the ground. Afterward the weather is usually warmer and more humid.

READING Diagrams

Write a paragraph comparing a warm front with a cold front.

Cold Front

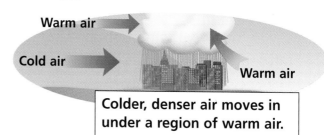

Colder, denser air moves in under a region of warm air.

Warm Front

Warm air moves into a region, rising up and over the colder air mass already there.

Why It Matters

Weather forecasting is hard. Knowing how the atmosphere is moving lets you predict the weather. The problem is that the atmosphere is huge and complex. A weather forecaster might predict clear weather for tomorrow. However, another air mass might move in. Everything can change.

Computers do high-speed calculations to predict the atmosphere's motion. Predictions are compared with forecasts to account for any differences. Two-day forecasts are calculated every 12 hours. A five-day forecast is calculated daily.

e-Journal Visit our Web site **www.science.mmhschool.com** to do a research project on weather forecasting.

Think and Write

1. What are four different kinds of air masses? How are they different?

2. What kind of weather is produced by a cold front?

3. What kind of weather is produced by a warm front?

4. How can you use weather maps to predict weather?

5. **Critical Thinking** How can you tell the kind of front passing by just observing the weather?

L·I·N·K·S

WRITING LINK

Expository Writing Write an interview for the local TV news. Explain how changes in the weather affected the way three people spent their day.

MATH LINK

Graph weather data. Research local newspapers to learn what kinds of fronts have moved through your area and the kind of weather each front brought. Do this for a month. Graph your data. Report what you found.

TECHNOLOGY LINK

 Science Newsroom CD-ROM Choose *It's Up in the Air* to learn more about how air masses affect weather conditions.

 LOG ON Visit **www.science.mmhschool.com** for more links.

Severe Storms

Vocabulary

thunderstorm, D76
tornado, D77
hurricane, D78
storm surge, D79

Get Ready

What's it like to be in the path of a tornado? People have reported a sound like the rumble of an approaching freight train. Tornadoes are the most powerful storms on Earth. Although most tornadoes are not very wide and they don't last too long, when they touch down watch out! Like deadly whirling brooms, they can sweep away anything in their path. Tornadoes strike all parts of the United States, but they are more frequent in some regions than in others. Where in the United States is "tornado country"?

Inquiry Skill

You use numbers when you use ordering, counting, adding, subtracting, multiplying, and dividing to explain data.

Explore Activity

Where Do Tornadoes Occur?

Materials

map of U.S., including Alaska and Hawaii

blue marker

red marker

Procedure

1 **Infer** The table shown here lists how many tornadoes occurred in each state over a 30-year period. It also shows about how many tornadoes occur in each state each year. Look at the data in the table for two minutes. Now write what part of the country you think gets the most tornadoes.

2 Use the red marker to record on the map the number of tornadoes that occurred in each state over the 30-year period. Use the blue marker to record the average number of tornadoes that occurred in a year in each state.

Drawing Conclusions

1 **Use Numbers** Which states had fewer than 10 tornadoes a year? Which states had more than 20 tornadoes a year?

2 **Interpret Data** Which six states had the most tornadoes during the 30-year period?

3 **Interpret Data** Which part of the country had the most tornadoes?

4 FURTHER INQUIRY **Communicate** Many people refer to a certain part of the country as "Tornado Alley." Which part of the country do you think that is? Why do you think people call it that? What else might these states have in common? Describe how you would go about finding the answer to that question.

State	Total	Average per year
AL	668	22
AK	0	0
AZ	106	4
AR	596	20
CA	148	5
CO	781	26
CT	37	1
DE	31	1
FL	1,590	53
GA	615	21
HI	25	1
ID	80	3
IL	798	27
IN	604	20
IA	1,079	36
KS	1,198	40
KY	296	10
LA	831	28
ME	50	2
MD	86	3
MA	89	3
MI	567	19
MN	607	20
MS	775	26
MO	781	26
MT	175	6
NE	1,118	37
NV	41	1
NH	56	2
NJ	78	3
NM	276	9
NY	169	6
NC	435	15
ND	621	21
OH	463	15
OK	1,412	47
OR	34	1
PA	310	10
RI	7	0
SC	307	10
SD	864	29
TN	360	12
TX	4,174	139
UT	58	2
VT	21	1
VA	188	6
WA	45	2
WV	69	2
WI	625	21
WY	356	12

Main Idea Thunderstorms, tornadoes, and hurricanes are severe storms that can cause great damage.

What Are Thunderstorms?

A tornado is a violent kind of storm that forms under special conditions. Often, such storms grow out of a **thunderstorm**, another, more common kind of storm.

Thunderstorms are the most common kind of severe storm. They form in clouds called *thunderheads*, or cumulonimbus clouds. The storms cause huge electric sparks called *lightning*. The lightning heats the air and causes the noise called *thunder*. Thunderstorms usually have heavy rains and strong winds. Some thunderstorms also produce hail. A thunderstorm starts when intense heating causes air to rise very quickly. A cloud forms where there is an upward rush of heated air, an updraft. As more warm, moist air is carried upward, the cloud grows larger. Strong updrafts keep water droplets and ice crystals in the cloud, so they grow in size, too. When the updrafts can't support them anymore, they fall as heavy rain or even hail.

Once the rain falls, it causes downdrafts in the cloud. When the air going up rubs against air going down, static electricity builds up. When enough builds up, there's a huge spark—lightning. Lightning may jump within a cloud, between two clouds, or between a cloud and the ground.

Thunderstorms usually form in warm air just ahead of a cold front. They most often occur in hot humid weather, but can also occur during snow storms, as *thundersnow*.

How a Thunderstorm Forms

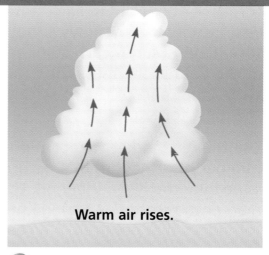

Warm air rises.

1 Strong updrafts form inside the cloud.

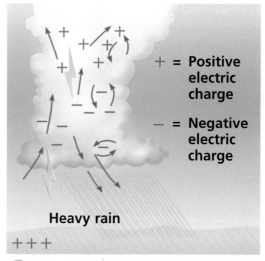

+ = Positive electric charge

− = Negative electric charge

Heavy rain

2 Electric charges build up inside the cloud.

READING
Diagrams

Describe how a thunderstorm forms.

The most violent thunderstorms often spin off even more dangerous storms, called **tornadoes**. A tornado is a violent whirling wind that moves across the ground in a narrow path.

How Tornadoes Happen

Late in the day, when Earth's surface is very warm, convection can get very strong. This can lead to a tornado. A tornado is a sort of runaway convection cell.

When the updraft in a convection cell is really strong, the air rushes in from all sides at high speeds. The air curves into a spin. This lowers the pressure even more. Air rushes in even faster, and the pressure gets even lower, and so on. Like a spinning skater who pulls her arms in close to her sides, the spinning tornado gets faster and faster.

As the tornado gets stronger, a funnel forms that eventually touches the ground. In the center of a tornado, winds can reach speeds of 500 km per hour (about 300 mi per hour) or more. At such high speeds, winds can destroy anything in their path.

The speed of the wind in the tornado is not the speed with which the tornado moves across the ground. It moves across the ground very fast but can change its direction continually.

Most tornadoes in the United States occur in the Midwest and the South—especially in the area known as Tornado Alley.

▷ **How are tornadoes related to thunderstorms?**

QUICK LAB

Tornado in a Bottle

FOLDABLES™ Make a Half-Book. (See p. R 41.)

1. **Make a Model** Fill a 2-L plastic bottle one-third full of water. Dry the neck of the bottle, and tape over the top with duct tape. Use a pencil to poke a hole in the tape.

2. Place another 2-L plastic bottle upside down over the mouth of the first bottle. Tape the two bottles together.

3. **Observe** Hold the bottles by the necks so the one with the water is on top. Swirl them around while your partner gently squeezes on the empty bottle. Then place the bottles on a desk with the water bottle on top. Draw what you see on the front of your book and describe your observations under the tab.

4. **Infer** How is this like what happens when a tornado forms? Explain.

How Do Hurricanes Form?

If you live near an ocean or the Gulf Coast, you may have experienced a **hurricane**. Hurricanes are very large, swirling storms with very low pressure at their center. They form over tropical oceans near the equator.

Air masses near the equator tend to be very much alike. They don't form the fronts that you learned about in Lesson 7. Instead, they form lots of thunderstorms.

- Strong heating and lots of evaporation over the ocean can cause a large low-pressure center to form. If this happens, winds begin to blow in toward the low. As this rushing air nears the center, it moves upward and forms a ring of tall thunderstorms.

- The Coriolis effect causes winds to spiral counterclockwise in the Northern Hemisphere. Clusters of thunderstorms are pulled into the spiral. The thunderstorms merge, forming a single large storm.

- As water vapor in the storms condenses, heat is released. The air is

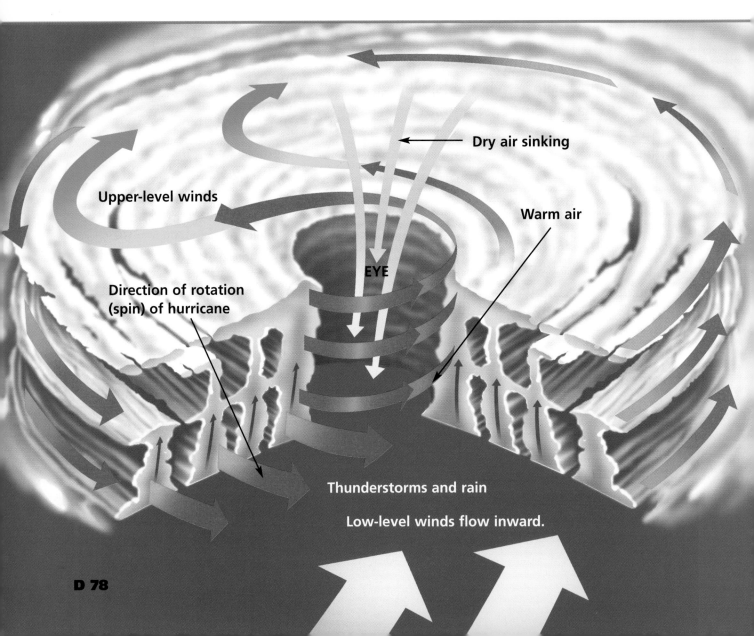

Dry air sinking

Upper-level winds

Warm air

EYE

Direction of rotation (spin) of hurricane

Thunderstorms and rain

Low-level winds flow inward.

warmed. This decreases the air's density and pressure. Moisture evaporating into the air decreases the air's density and pressure even more. Low air pressure favors more evaporation. This lowers the pressure even more.

- The lower the air pressure, the faster are the winds that blow in toward the center of the storm. When the winds reach speeds of 120 km per hour (about 75 mi per hour) or higher, the storm is a hurricane.

- As the moist air in the storm rises and cools, condensation takes place. The clouds thicken. Heavy rains fall through the high winds. When fully formed, a hurricane has an eye at its center. The eye is an area of light winds and skies that are nearly clear.

Hurricane winds whip up large waves in the ocean. These waves move outward from the storm and pound against a shore for days before the storm arrives. However, it is the **storm surge** that causes the most destruction. Storm surge is a great rise of the sea along a shore. Its main cause is low air pressure.

Air pressure normally presses down on the surface of the sea. When the pressure drops in a hurricane, the surface of the sea rises, forming a bulge beneath a hurricane.

When the hurricane moves over a coast, the bulge can cause water levels to suddenly rise several feet, or surge.

Hurricane winds also push water ahead of the storm, forcing water onshore and adding to the storm surge. If the storm surge comes at high tide, it can raise the water level by 7 meters (about 20 feet) or more.

READING **Sequence of Events**
How does lower and lower air pressure lead to the formation of a hurricane?

This satellite photograph shows a hurricane and its eye. Hurricanes can easily grow to more than 700 km (about 400 mi) in diameter. Hurricanes can pick up about 20 billion tons of water a day from the oceans. Much of this water falls as rain over land areas.

Direction of wind

How Can Radar Track Storms?

Storms are hard to predict because they form so quickly. Scientists use the best methods possible to try to identify conditions long before a storm occurs. They look for clues, like the movement of fronts and the formation of very low pressure areas. Once these conditions are located, scientists keep a "weather eye" on them to see how they develop.

Special methods are used to find storms as they form. One such method is Doppler radar. The word *radar* stands for *ra*dio *d*etection *a*nd *r*anging. Radar works by sending out radio waves and recording their echo. The change in the radio signal from the original to the echo tells us something about where it reflected.

Doppler radar looks at how the echoes have changed in frequency from the original signals. This information gives clues about the movement of the reflective surface. Doppler radar is a very good tool for scientists to track storms. The radio waves reflect off storm clouds and are picked back up again at the radar stations.

With Doppler radar scientists can tell if rain is moving toward or away from them. Doppler radar can also spot spinning motions of clouds. These motions help warn scientists that tornadoes or hurricanes may be forming. Scientists use Doppler radar to find and track thunderstorms, tornadoes, and hurricanes. Doppler radar helps forecasters predict which way the storms will travel.

▷ **How can Doppler radar help in predicting severe storms?**

Radar helps forecasters watch how storms form and move.

Why It Matters

Scientists have used radar systems to track storms since the 1950s. NEXRAD—"NEXt generation of weather RADar"—is a newer form of Doppler radar that is replacing older radar systems. NEXRAD can spot small particles such as blowing dust, very light snow, and even drizzle. NEXRAD is more accurate than conventional radar at predicting floods and flash floods. It can show the exact locations of different fronts. It also shows changes in wind speed and direction. This helps scientists make more accurate weather predictions.

e-Journal Visit our Web site www.science.mmhschool.com to do a research project on storms.

Think and Write

1. How does a thunderstorm form?

2. How is a tornado related to a thunderstorm?

3. What causes a hurricane to form? What makes its winds move in a certain direction?

4. Why can hurricanes cause so much damage?

5. **Critical Thinking** Why do you think predicting a severe storm is so difficult?

WRITING LINK

Explanatory Writing How can you stay safe during an ice storm or a blizzard? Research the ways. Then use the information you find to write a safety manual on how to stay safe during these storms. Include an illustration for each step you list. Be that your safety manual tells people what to do first, next, and last.

ART LINK

Make a poster. Let others know what to do in a thunderstorm, tornado, or hurricane. Make a poster illustrating important storm safety rules.

MATH LINK

Find the number of tornadoes. Research how many tornadoes hit your state in the past year. Compare that number with the average number listed for your state in the chart on page D75. Were the number of tornadoes in your state last year higher, lower, or the same as the listed average?

TECHNOLOGY LINK

LOG ON Visit www.science.mmhschool.com for more links.

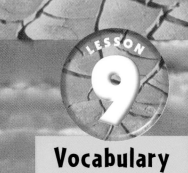

Climate

Get Ready

What if you lived here, in this desert? What would summers be like? What would winters be like?

Think about what factors are used to describe the average weather pattern of a region. How might you use graphs of year-round weather in different places to test your ideas?

Inquiry Skill

You **communicate when you share information.**

Explore Activity

What Do Weather Patterns Tell You?

Procedure

1 **Use Numbers** Look at the graph for City 1. The bottom is labeled with the months of the year. The left side is labeled with the temperature in degrees Celsius. Use this scale to read the temperature line. What is City 1's average temperature in July?

2 **Use Numbers** The right side of the graph shows millimeters (mm) of precipitation. Use this scale to read precipitation bars. What is City 1's average precipitation in July?

3 Repeat steps 1 and 2 for City 2.

Drawing Conclusions

1 **Use Numbers** How does the annual precipitation of the two cities compare?

2 **Interpret Data** When is the average temperature highest for each city? Lowest? When does each city receive the greatest amount of precipitation?

3 **Interpret Data** Describe the average weather pattern for each city. Be sure to include temperature and precipitation, and their relationship to the seasons.

4 FURTHER INQUIRY **Communicate** What would a yearly graph for your community look like? Gather monthly temperature and precipitation data. Construct your graph. Compare it to City 1 and City 2.

City 1

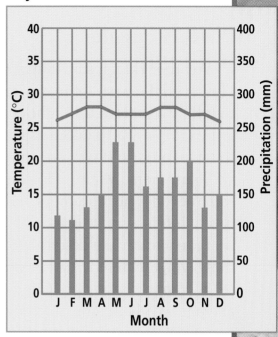

City 2

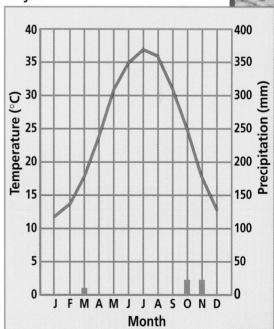

— Temperature (in Celsius)
■ Precipitation (in millimeters)

Main Idea Long-term weather patterns determine climates, which can change over time.

What Is Climate?

Weather changes from day to day. However, the weather in any area tends to follow a pattern throughout the year. For example, Fairbanks, Alaska, tends to have long, cold winters and short, cool summers. Miami, Florida, tends to have long, hot summers and short, cool winters.

When you make descriptions such as these, you are describing the **climate** (KLIGH·mit) of a region. Climate is the average weather pattern of a region. One way to describe a region's climate is with a temperature-precipitation graph.

The climate of a region can also be described by some other factors, such as winds, distance from a coast, mountain ranges, and ocean currents. The *climate zones* shown here take all these factors into account.

Another way to describe the climate of a region is by the plants that grow there, such as grasslands or coniferous forests. Each kind of plant requires its own conditions for growth, such as amount of sunlight, precipitation, and temperature.

> ▷ **What factors describe climate?**

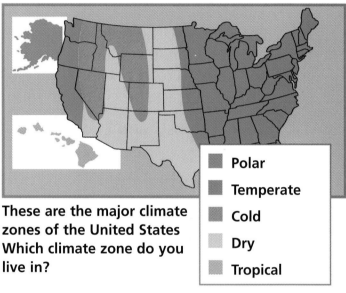

These are the major climate zones of the United States Which climate zone do you live in?

- Polar
- Temperate
- Cold
- Dry
- Tropical

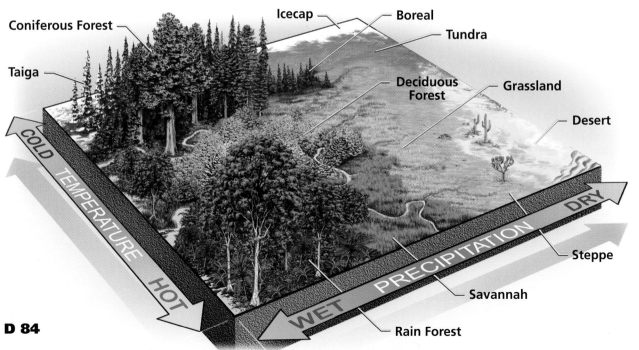

Coniferous Forest

Icecap — Boreal

Taiga — Tundra

Deciduous Forest — Grassland

Desert

COLD

TEMPERATURE

HOT

WET

PRECIPITATION

DRY

Steppe

Savannah

Rain Forest

Inquiry Skill
BUILDER

Modeling Climates

In this activity you will make a model of the soil conditions in two cities. Use the information in the graphs on page D83. The soil conditions you set up will model—or represent—the climates of the two cities. To do this, you will need to measure the amount of water you use and the amount of time you use the lamp.

Procedure

1 **Measure** Put 3 cm of dry soil into each tray. Label one tray City 1 and the other tray City 2.

2 **Use Numbers** What do the bars on each graph represent?

3 **Measure** Model the yearly precipitation and temperature like this: Let 5 minutes equal 1 month. One squeeze of water sprayed on the tray equals 10 millimeters of precipitation. Every minute the lamp is on equals 20 degrees of temperature. That means that from 0 to 5 minutes is January. During January the City 2 tray gets no water and the lamp shines on it for $\frac{3}{4}$ minute. The City 1 tray gets 12 squeezes of water and the lamp shines on it for $1\frac{1}{4}$ minutes.

4 **Make a Model** Model the two cities for all 12 months. Record your observations.

Drawing Conclusions

1 **Observe** Examine the soil in the trays. Compare them for the same months. How do they differ?

2 **Communicate** How did measuring help you model climates?

Materials

stick-on notepaper

marking pencil or pen

2 trays of dry soil

spray bottle of water

lamp

thermometer

What Affects Climate?

Several things affect temperature and precipitation over a long period of time.

Latitude

One way to describe location is to tell the latitude of a place. Latitude is a measure of how far north or south a place is from the equator. The angle of insolation is different at different latitudes. As a result, the temperatures are different at different latitudes.

- **Tropical Zone** Near the equator temperatures are high all year. Rainfall is plentiful. At about 30° latitude in each hemisphere are deserts, areas of high temperatures and low precipitation.

- **Temperate Zones** In the middle latitudes, summers are warm, and winters are cool or cold. Precipitation may be plentiful.

- **Polar Zones** At high latitudes winters are long and cold. Summers are short and warm. Precipitation all year is low.

Bodies of Water

A glance at any globe shows that land and water are not evenly distributed. Most of the globe is covered with water. However, some places on a continent can be more than 1,600 km (1,000 mi) from any large body of water. Land and water heat and cool at different rates. Land heats up faster in the sunlight than water does. Land also cools off faster than water. As a result, air temperatures over land are warmer in summer and cooler in winter than they are over oceans at the same latitude.

Winds and Ocean Currents

In Lesson 6 you learned that wind patterns circle the globe. These patterns are not the day-to-day winds. Instead they are winds that blow continually above Earth's surface.

- **Wind Patterns** For example, just above and below the equator, the trade winds blow continually. In the middle latitudes are the westerlies. In the polar areas are the easterlies. Westerlies blow across the continental United States from west (the Pacific) to east (the Atlantic). They bring warm, moist air to the west coast. They push air masses and fronts across the country.

North Pole

Polar zone — Sparse precipitation

Temperate zone — Ample precipitation

Tropical zone — Abundant rainfall

Temperate zone — Ample precipitation

Polar zone — Sparse precipitation

South Pole

- **Currents** These winds also move water across the surface of the ocean. As ocean water moves, it moves warm or cool air with it. A warm current, the Gulf Stream, flows up along the east coast. The California Current, a cool current, moves down along the west coast.

Altitude

Altitude is a measure of how high above sea level a place is. The higher a place is above sea level, the cooler its climate is.

- **Mountains** Along the base of a high mountain, you may find tropical plants growing. Halfway up you might find pine forests. At the mountain peaks, you will find permanent ice and snow. Mountain ranges affect climate, too. The Alps protect the Mediterranean coast from cold polar air. The Himalayas protect the lowlands of India from cold Siberian air. Mountain ranges also affect rain patterns. Often one side of the mountain gets lots of rain while the other side gets very little.

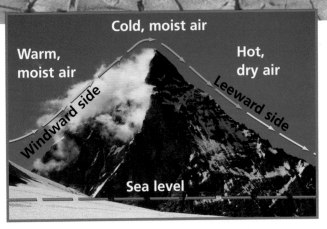

Air passing over a mountain cools. Rain clouds may form and drop their moisture on that side of the mountain. Air reaching the other side is often dry.

- **Rain Shadow** Global wind patterns can force air up along the side of a mountain. For example, warm, moist air from the Pacific Ocean is blown up the side of the Sierra Nevada and the Cascades. As the air moves up, there is precipitation on the windward side. Having lost the moisture, dry air descends down the leeward side of the mountain. This side is said to be in a *rain shadow.*

▶ **How does latitude affect climate?**

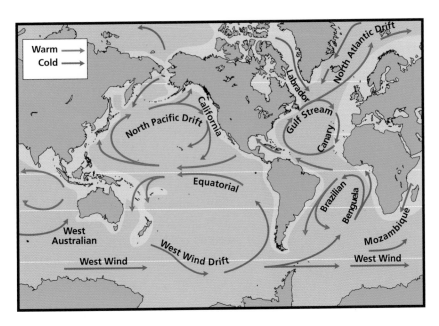

Ocean currents move surface water in huge circular patterns. As ocean currents flow past land areas, they affect the land's climate.

What Causes Climate Change?

There is much evidence that over long periods of time, Earth goes through warming and cooling trends. Warming and cooling are signs that Earth's radiative (energy) balance has shifted. What causes such shifts?

The shifts are caused by changes in sunlight. They are also caused by changes in the movements of air, water, landmasses, and Earth itself.

The Sun's Output

The amount of energy the Sun sends out changes. One clue to how the Sun's output may be changing comes from sunspots. Sunspots are dark areas that appear on the surface of the Sun. They appear dark because they are cooler than the surrounding regions. They appear to be "storms" on the Sun.

Sunspots have been observed for centuries. However, they are not permanent. They appear and disappear over several days or several months.

At times there are many large sunspots. Such a high count is called a *sunspot maximum*. The last sunspot maximum was in 2001.

A sunspot maximum appears to happen about every 11 years. Scientists also record changes in Earth's temperatures about the same times. Around the time of a sunspot maximum, Earth's average temperature has gone up. The pattern is not exact or complete. However, it has led some scientists to suggest that droughts, rainfall, and very cold winters might be related to times when sunspots are very numerous or very few.

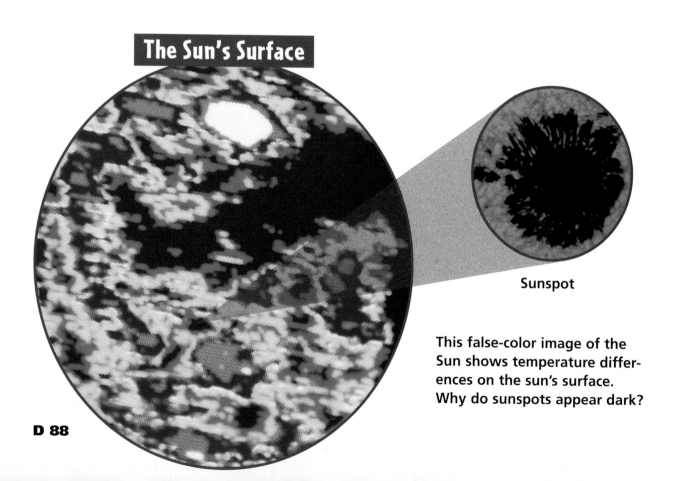

The Sun's Surface

Sunspot

This false-color image of the Sun shows temperature differences on the sun's surface. Why do sunspots appear dark?

Currents and Landmasses

How do the oceans help move Earth's heat around? Ocean currents act like huge conveyor belts, carrying heat from the equator to the poles. Changes in the speed and direction of these currents could explain sudden and long-term climate changes.

The continents have changed their positions over time. In fact, the continents are still moving very gradually. Their climates are likely to change with their locations.

Volcanoes

When volcanoes erupt, they send dust and gases into the atmosphere. Atmospheric dust can block sunlight, causing cooling. In the past eruptions were more frequent. The dust from all of those eruptions may have caused enough cooling to trigger ice ages. Volcanic eruptions are not as common today as they were in the past. While eruptions still cause cooling, they probably don't affect long-term climate as much as in the past.

READING Sequence of Events

How might frequent volcanic eruptions change the climate?

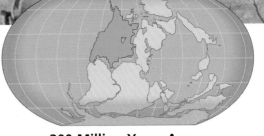

300 Million Years Ago

Present

Do you think the ocean currents were the same 300 million years ago as they are today? Changes in ocean currents would profoundly affect climates.

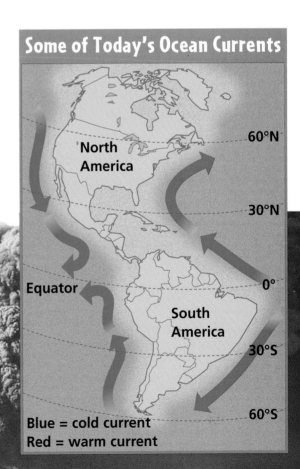

Some of Today's Ocean Currents

North America

60°N

30°N

Equator

0°

South America

30°S

60°S

Blue = cold current
Red = warm current

How Can Climate Affect You?

How do you deal with cold weather? Cold weather cools the surface of the body. The body responds by circulating warm blood faster to counteract the cooling. The heart pumps faster. Blood pressure increases and puts a strain on the heart.

Cold Climates

How can you stay warm in cold weather? Use proper clothing and shelter. Clothing traps body heat to warm the air close to your body. Cold-weather clothes are often made with materials that trap air between loose fibers. Dressing in layers helps. Your body heats trapped air, and soon a thin, warm layer of air surrounds you.

Hot Climates

In hot, dry climates, the main health problem is water loss. Heating the body triggers sweating. When sweat evaporates, it cools the skin. However, if you don't drink enough water, your body eventually stops sweating. No sweat, no cooling. Body temperature rises. This can cause *hyperthermia* (overheating), which can be fatal.

Clothing can help you deal with the heat. Light-colored fabric protects the skin and reflects a lot of the sunlight. Loose clothing lets air circulate so sweat can evaporate and cool the body.

▷ **What is the main health problem in hot, dry climates?**

How to Dress in Hot Weather
Wear light-colored, loose clothing that protects you from the Sun and lets your skin breathe.
Wear a sun hat.
Use sunscreen.

How to Dress in Cold Weather
Protect nose and ears on blustery, cold days.
Keep hands, head, and feet warm.
Dress in layers to trap body heat.

Why It Matters

Since 1900, Earth's average temperature has increased by about 0.5°C (1°F). Most of the warming has come in two periods—from 1920 to 1940 and since the mid-1970s. A drought during the 1920s–1940s led to the Dust Bowl days. Millions of acres of United States farmland dried out. Crops failed. Farmers went broke trying to pay their bills. Many families lost their homes and farms.

Today the warming trend continues.

e-Journal Visit our Web site www.science.mmhschool.com to do a research project on global warming.

Think and Write

1. What is climate? What are the main factors that are used to describe the climate of an area?

2. What is a rain shadow?

3. Why are climates different at different places on Earth?

4. **Measure** What variables do you have to measure to describe the average weather pattern, or climate, of a region?

5. **Critical Thinking** Do you think people can live in all climates? Explain your answer.

WRITING LINK

Persuasive Writing "Greenhouse gases" in the atmosphere let in sunlight, but trap heat. Research what these gases are and how they affect Earth's climate. Write a letter to a politician. Convince this person to pass a law preventing people from placing these gases into the atmosphere.

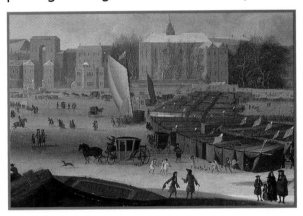

SOCIAL STUDIES LINK

Report on changing climates. The illustration shows a winter fair on the Thames River in England during the Little Ice Age. Research how Earth's climate changed since farming began. Write a report.

MATH LINK

Make a pie graph. Find out what proportions of greenhouse gases exist in the atmosphere. Make a pie graph.

TECHNOLOGY LINK

LOG ON Visit www.science.mmhschool.com for more links.

Chapter 11 Review

Vocabulary

Fill each blank with the best word or words from the list.

air mass, D70
climate, D84
cold front, D72
front, D71
hurricane, D78
lightning, D76
storm surge, D79
thunderstorm, D76
tornado, D77
warm front, D72

1. A boundary between air masses of different temperatures is called a(n) _____.

2. A storm often created in thunderstorms is a(n) _____.

3. A(n) _____ may bring fog.

4. A storm that produces lightning is a(n) _____.

5. A great rise of sea level at a shore due to a hurricane is a(n) _____.

6. Thunderstorms cause large electric sparks called _____.

7. A large region of the atmosphere in which the air has similar properties is a(n) _____.

8. A dangerous storm that forms over warm ocean waters is a(n) _____.

9. A(n) _____ forms when cold air moves in under a warm air mass.

10. The average weather pattern of a region is its _____.

Test Prep

11. Thunderheads are also known as _____.
   A cumulus clouds
   B cumulonimbus clouds
   C stratus clouds
   D cirrus clouds

12. Winds curve to the right in the northern hemisphere because of the _____.
   F Coriolis Effect
   G relative humidity
   H Sun
   J Moon

13. A _____ usually brings cooler, drier air.
   A warm front
   B humid day
   C storm surge
   D cold front

14. The side of a mountain that usually does not get rain is _____.

    F in a rain shadow

    G facing the Pacific coast

    H on the windward side

    J facing the wind

15. A hurricane can cause sea level to rise because the air pressure under the hurricane _____.

    A is higher than normal

    B is lower than normal

    C is the same as usual

    D does not affect why a hurricane makes the sea level rise

Concepts and Skills

16. Reading in Science Write a paragraph explaining how a thunderstorm forms.

17. Scientific Methods Design a research project to determine whether sunspot activity affects Earth's climate.

18. Product Ads What products are advertised to protect you from the weather in the winter? In the summer? What is each product supposed to do? Are the products as good as the ads say? Write a paragraph explaining your answer.

19. INQUIRY SKILL **Measure** What if your area were to get twice as much rain as usual for the next ten years? Write a paragraph explaining how you would make a model of your climate as it is now. How would you adjust it to study the effect of extra rainfall?

20. Critical Thinking Do you think that Earth is getting warmer? Write a paragraph explaining your hypothesis. Describe what you might do to test your ideas.

Did You Ever Wonder?

INQUIRY SKILL **Form a hypothesis** Are cities warmer than their surrounding areas? How can you test this?

LOG ON Visit www.science.mmhschool.com to boost your test scores.

Tim Samaras

TORNADO CHASER

Tornadoes are nature's most powerful storms. They can produce winds that blow at speeds of 300 miles an hour. Tornadoes can destroy homes and kill people. Sometimes people don't have enough warning that a tornado is headed their way. That's where tornado chasers come in. They work to give scientists information to develop warning systems.

Tim Samaras looks for a storm that he thinks will spin off a tornado. Once he spots a tornado, Samaras does the opposite of what most people do. He drives his minivan *toward* the storm to study it.

Inside his minivan are instruments to record weather and wind data. There is also a powerful computer with mapping software to track the storm.

Samaras has also created a tough instrument, or probe. It takes readings from *inside* a tornado. Getting a probe inside a tornado is tricky. Tornadoes don't follow straight paths, so it's hard to guess where they will head next.

In May 2002, near Dodge City, Kansas, Samaras placed a probe in a spot where he hoped a twister would hit. Later, Samaras recovered the probe. It had been inside the twister! The probe had recorded barometric pressure, wind speed, and temperature.

Thanks to the work of storm chasers, scientists are learning why some storms produce tornadoes. They also can be more certain of where a tornado will form. With this information, they are improving storm prediction and saving lives.

Tim Samaras in the field

TOP 5 Worst Years for Tornadoes

The United States has more tornadoes than any other country—about 1,000 a year. Each year, about 38 tornadoes get rated very strong to violent on a scale of wind speed.

1. 1975: 116 strong tornadoes
2. 1965: 75 strong tornadoes
3. 1957: 64 strong tornadoes
4. 1973 and 1976: 59 strong tornadoes
5. 1971: 56 strong tornadoes

Write About It

1. Why is it hard to place a probe in the path of a tornado?
2. Why is the work of storm chasers important?

LOG ON Visit www.science.mmhschool.com to learn more about storm chasers and tornadoes.

Performance Assessment

Football-Field Solar System

Your goal is to make a model of the solar system.

What to Do

Use the data tables from the Explore activity on page D15 and from the Inquiry Skill Builder on page D17.

Explain how you would make a model solar system on a 100-yard football field, if you placed your model Sun at one end and your model Earth two yards away. Include approximate positions for the asteroid belt, the Kuiper Belt, and the Oort Cloud.

Analyze Your Results

1. Where would Jupiter be placed? Where would Pluto be placed?

2. Approximately where would you place the asteroid belt? Where would you place the Kuiper Belt? The Oort cloud?

3. What else would you have to do if you wanted to make a true scale model of the solar system?

CLIMATE on a CHART

Your goal is to make a climate chart of your local area.

What to Do

A climate chart shows average values for temperature (°C) and precipitation (mm). Use local data to make a climate chart for your area.

Analyze Your Results

1. What is the rainiest month where you live? The least rainy month?

2. What is the hottest month where you live? The coldest?

3. Describe your local climate in words based on your climate chart.

For Your Reference

Science Handbook

Health Handbook

Units of Measurement

Units of Measurement

This bottle of juice has a volume of 1 liter.

That is a little more than 1 quart.

She can walk 20 meters in 5 seconds.

That means her speed is 4 meters per second.

Table of Measurements

International System of Units (SI)	English System of Units
Temperature Water freezes at 0°C and boils at 100°C.	**Temperature** Water freezes at 32°F and boils at 212°F.
Length and Distance 1,000 meters (m) = 1 kilometer (km) 100 centimeters (cm) = 1 meter 10 millimeters (mm) = 1 centimeter	**Length and Distance** 5,280 feet = 1 mile 3 feet = 1 yard 12 inches = 1 foot
Volume 1,000 milliliters (mL) = 1 liter (L) 1 cubic centimeter (cm³) = 1 milliliter	**Volume of Fluids** 4 quarts = 1 gallon 2 pints = 1 quart 2 cups = 1 pint 8 fluid ounces = 1 cup
Mass 1,000 grams (g) = 1 kilogram (kg)	**Weight** 2,000 pounds = 1 ton 16 ounces = 1 pound

Use a Hand Lens

You use a hand lens to magnify an object, or make the object look larger. With a hand lens, you can see details that would be hard to see without the hand lens.

Magnify a Piece of Cereal

1. Place a piece of your favorite cereal on a flat surface. Look at the cereal carefully. Draw a picture of it.
2. Look at the cereal through the large lens of a hand lens. Move the lens toward or away from the cereal until it looks larger and in focus. Draw a picture of the cereal as you see it through the hand lens. Fill in details that you did not see before.
3. Look at the cereal through the smaller lens, which will magnify the cereal even more. If you notice more details, add them to your drawing.
4. Repeat this activity using objects you are studying in science. It might be a rock, some soil, or a seed.

Observe Seeds in a Petri Dish

Can you observe a seed as it sprouts? You can if it's in a petri dish. A petri dish is a shallow, clear, round dish with a cover.

1. Line the sides and bottom of a petri dish with a double layer of filter paper or paper towel. You may have to cut the paper to make it fit.
2. Sprinkle water on the paper to wet it.
3. Place three or four radish seeds on the wet paper in different areas of the dish. Put the lid on the dish, and keep it in a warm place.
4. Observe the seeds every day for a week. Use a hand lens to look for a tiny root pushing through the seed. Record how long it takes each seed to sprout.

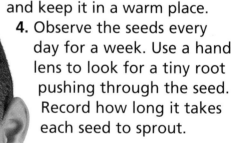

Collect Data

Use a Microscope

Hand lenses make objects look several times larger. A microscope, however, can magnify an object to look hundreds of times larger.

Examine Salt Grains

1. Look at the photograph to learn the different parts of your microscope.
2. Place the microscope on a flat surface. Always carry a microscope with both hands. Hold the arm with one hand, and put your other hand beneath the base.
3. Move the mirror so that it reflects light up toward the stage. Never point the mirror directly at the Sun or a bright light. Bright light can cause permanent eye damage.
4. Place a few grains of salt on the slide. Put the slide under the stage clips. Be sure that the salt grains you are going to examine are over the hole in the stage.
5. Look through the eyepiece. Turn the focusing knob slowly until the salt grains come into focus.
6. Draw what the grains look like through the microscope.
7. Look at other objects through the microscope. Try a piece of leaf, a human hair, or a pencil mark.

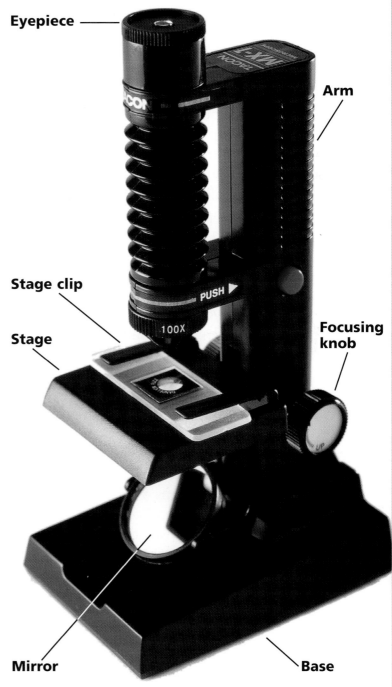

Eyepiece

Arm

Stage clip

PUSH ▶

100X

Stage

Focusing knob

Mirror

Base

Measure Time

You use timing devices to measure how long something takes to happen. Some timing devices you use in science are a clock with a second hand and a stopwatch. Which one is more accurate?

Comparing a Clock and Stopwatch

1. Look at a clock with a second hand. The second hand is the hand that you can see moving. It measures seconds.

2. Get an egg timer with falling sand or some device like a wind-up toy that runs down after a certain length of time. When the second hand of the clock points to 12, tell your partner to start the egg timer. Watch the clock while the sand in the egg timer is falling.

3. When the sand stops falling, count how many seconds it took. Record this measurement. Repeat the activity, and compare the two measurements.

4. Switch roles with your partner.

5. Look at a stopwatch. Click the button on the top right. This starts the time. Click the button again. This stops the time. Click the button on the top left. This sets the stopwatch back to zero. Notice that the stopwatch tells time in minutes, seconds, and hundredths of a second.

6. Repeat the activity in steps 1–3, using the stopwatch instead of a clock. Make sure the stopwatch is set to zero. Click the top right button to start timing the reading. Click it again when the sand stops falling. Make sure you and your partner time each other twice.

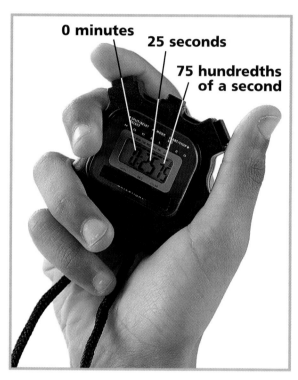

0 minutes   **25 seconds**   **75 hundredths of a second**

More About Time

1. Use the stopwatch to time how long it takes an ice cube to melt under cold running water. How long does an ice cube take to melt under warm running water?

2. Match each of these times with the action you think took that amount of time.

   a. 00:14:55
   b. 44:39:45
   c. 10:23:00

   1. Taking a shower
   2. Saying the Pledge of Allegiance
   3. Recess

Measure Length

Find Length with a Ruler

1. Look at this section of a ruler. Each centimeter is divided into 10 millimeters. How long is the paper clip?
2. The length of the paper clip is 3 centimeters plus 2 millimeters. You can write this length as 3.2 centimeters.
3. Place the ruler on your desk. Lay a pencil against the ruler so that one end of the pencil lines up with the left edge of the ruler. Record the length of the pencil.
4. Trade your pencil with a classmate. Measure and record the length of each other's pencil. Compare your answers.

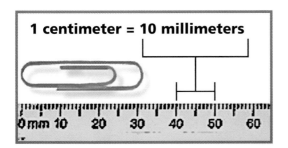

1 centimeter = 10 millimeters

Measuring Area

Area is the amount of surface something covers. To find the area of a rectangle, multiply the rectangle's length by its width. For example, the rectangle here is 3 centimeters long and 2 centimeters wide. Its area is 3 cm x 2 cm = 6 square centimeters. You write the area as 6 cm^2.

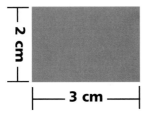

2 cm

3 cm

Opposite sides of a rectangle are parallel. The adjacent sides are perpendicular to each other (at right angles). Rectangles have symmetry. When folded in half, both halves are identical in size and shape. This is known as congruence. The two halves fit over each other exactly.

Find Length with a Meterstick

1. Line up the meterstick with the left edge of the chalkboard. Make a chalk mark on the board at the right end of the meterstick.
2. Move the meterstick so that the left edge lines up with the chalk mark. Keep the stick level. Make another mark on the board at the right end of the meterstick.
3. Continue to move the meterstick and make chalk marks until the meterstick meets or overlaps the right edge of the board.
4. Record the length of the chalkboard in centimeters by adding all the measurements you've made. Remember, a meterstick has 100 centimeters.

Estimating Length

Try estimating the length of objects in the room. Then measure the length, and compare the estimation with the measurement.

R 7

Measure Mass

Mass is the amount of matter an object has. You use a balance to measure mass. To find the mass of an object, you balance it with objects whose masses you know. Let's find the mass of a box of crayons.

Measure the Mass of a Box of Crayons

1. Place the balance on a flat, level surface. Check that the two pans are empty and clean.
2. Make sure the empty pans are balanced with each other. The pointer should point to the middle mark. If it does not, move the slider a little to the right or left to balance the pans.
3. Gently place a box of crayons on the left pan. This pan will drop lower.
4. Add masses to the right pan until the pans are balanced.
5. Add the numbers on the masses that are in the right pan. The total is the mass of the box of crayons, in grams. Record this number. After the number write a *g* for "grams."

Estimating Mass

Once you become familiar with the mass of objects, you can try estimating the masses of objects. Then you can compare the estimation with the actual mass.

More About Mass

The mass of your crayons was probably less than 100 grams. You may not have enough masses to balance a pineapple. It has a mass of about 1,000 grams. That's the same as 1 kilogram, because *kilo* means "1,000."

1. How many kilograms do all these masses add up to?
2. Which of these objects have a mass greater than 1 kilogram?

Make Measurements

Measure Volume

Volume is the amount of space something takes up. In science you usually measure the volume of liquids by using beakers and graduated cylinders. These containers are marked in milliliters (mL).

Measure the Volume of a Liquid

1. Look at the beaker and at the graduated cylinder. The beaker has marks for each 25 mL up to 200 mL. The graduated cylinder has marks for each 1 mL up to 100 mL.
2. The surface of the water in the graduated cylinder curves up at the sides. You measure the volume by reading the height of the water at the flat part. What is the volume of water in the graduated cylinder? How much water is in the beaker? They both contain 75 mL of water.
3. Pour 50 mL of water from a pitcher into a beaker.
4. Now pour the 50 mL of water into a graduated cylinder.

Find the Volume of a Solid

Here's a way to find the volume of a solid, such as a rock.

1. Start with 50 mL of water in a graduated cylinder.
2. Place a small rock in the water. The water level rises.
3. Measure the new water level. Subtract 50 mL from the new reading. The difference is the volume of the rock. Record the volume in cm³.

Estimating Volume

Once you become familiar with the volumes of liquids and solids, you can estimate volumes. Estimate the amount of liquid in a glass or can. Estimate the volume of an eraser.

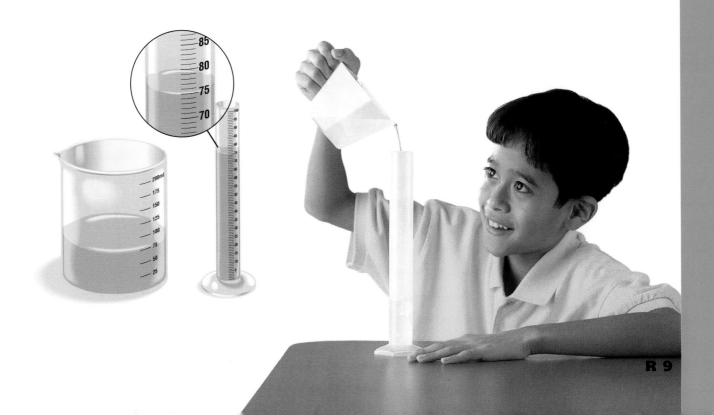

Measure Weight/Force

You use a spring scale to measure weight. An object has weight because the force of gravity pulls down on the object. Therefore, weight is a force. Weight is measured in newtons (N) like all forces.

Measure the Weight of an Object

1. Look at your spring scale to see how many newtons it measures. See how the measurements are divided. The spring scale shown here measures up to 5 N. It has a mark for every 0.1 N.
2. Hold the spring scale by the top loop. Put the object to be measured on the bottom hook. If the object will not stay on the hook, place it in a net bag. Then hang the bag from the hook.
3. Let go of the object slowly. It will pull down on a spring inside the scale. The spring is connected to a pointer. The pointer on the spring scale shown here is a small bar.
4. Wait for the pointer to stop moving. Read the number of newtons next to the pointer. This is the object's weight. The mug in the picture weighs 4 N.

More About Spring Scales

You probably weigh yourself by standing on a bathroom scale. This is a spring scale. The force of your body stretches a spring inside the scale. The dial on the scale is probably marked in pounds—the English unit of weight. One pound is equal to about 4.5 newtons.

A bathroom scale, a grocery scale, and a kitchen scale are some other spring scales you may have seen.

Measure Temperature

You use a thermometer to measure temperature—how hot or cold something is. A thermometer is made of a thin tube with colored liquid inside. When the liquid gets warmer, it expands and moves up the tube. When the liquid gets cooler, it contracts and moves down the tube. You may have seen most temperatures measured in degrees Fahrenheit (°F). Scientists measure temperature in degrees Celsius (°C).

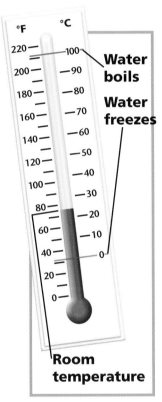

°F °C

Water boils

Water freezes

Room temperature

Read a Thermometer

1. Look at the thermometer shown here. It has two scales—a Fahrenheit scale and a Celsius scale.
2. What is the temperature shown on the thermometer? At what temperature does water freeze?

What Is Convection?

1. Fill a large beaker about two-thirds full of cool water. Find the temperature of the water by holding a thermometer in the water. Do not let the bulb at the bottom of the thermometer touch the sides or bottom of the beaker.
2. Keep the thermometer in the water until the liquid in the tube stops moving—about 1 minute. Read and record the temperature in °C.
3. Sprinkle a little fish food on the surface of the water in the beaker. Do

not knock the beaker, and most of the food will stay on top.

4. Carefully place the beaker on a hot plate. A hot plate is a small electric stove. Plug in the hot plate, and turn the control knob to a middle setting.
5. After 1 minute measure the temperature of water near the bottom of the beaker. At the same time, a classmate should measure the temperature of water near the top of the beaker. Record these temperatures. Is water near the bottom of the beaker heating up faster than near the top?
6. As the water heats up, notice what happens to the fish food. How do you know that warmer water at the bottom of the beaker rises and cooler water at the top sinks?

Use Calculators

Sometimes after you make measurements, you have to analyze your data to see what it means. This might involve doing calculations with your data. A calculator helps you do time-consuming calculations.

Find an Average

After you collect a set of measurements, you may want to get an idea of a typical measurement in that set. What if, for example, you are doing a weather project? As part of the project, you are studying rainfall data of a nearby town. The table shows how much rain fell in that town each week during the summer.

Week	Rain (cm)
1	2.0
2	1.4
3	0.0
4	0.5
5	1.2
6	2.5
7	1.8
8	1.4
9	2.4
10	8.6
11	7.5

What if you want to get an idea of how much rain fell during a typical week in the summer? In other words, you want to find the average for the set of data. There are three kinds of averages—mean, median, and mode. Does it matter which one you use?

Find the Mean

The mean is what most people think of when they hear the word *average*. You can use a calculator to find the mean.

1. Make sure the calculator is on.
2. Add the numbers. To add a series of numbers, enter the first number and press ⊞. Repeat until you enter the last number. See the hints below. After your last number, press ⌹. Your total should be 29.3.
3. While entering so many numbers, it's easy to make a mistake and hit the wrong key. If you make a mistake, correct it by pressing the clear entry key, CE. Then continue entering the rest of the numbers.
4. Find the mean by dividing your total by the number of weeks. If 29.3 is displayed, press ÷ 1 1 ⌹. Rounded up to one decimal point, your mean should be 2.7.

Hints:
- If the only number to the right of the decimal point is 0, you don't have to enter it into the calculator. To enter 2.0, just press 2.
- If the only number to the left of the decimal point is 0, you don't have to enter it into the calculator. To enter 0.5, just press . 5.

Use Technology

Find the Median

The median is the middle number when the numbers are arranged in order of size. When the rainfall measurements are arranged in order of size, they look like this.

0.0
0.5
1.2
1.4
1.4
1.8 ———— The median is 1.8. This number is in the middle; there are five numbers above it and five numbers below it.
2.0
2.4
2.5
7.5
8.6

Find the Mode

The mode is the number that occurs most frequently. From the ranked set of data above, you can see that the most frequent number is 1.4. It occurs twice. Here are your three different averages from the same set of data.

Average Weekly Rainfall (cm)

Mean	2.7
Median	1.8
Mode	1.4

Why is the mean so much higher than the median or mode? The mean is affected greatly by the last two weeks when it rained a lot. A typical week for that summer was much drier than either of those last two weeks. The median or mode gives a better idea of rainfall for a typical week.

Find the Percent

Sometimes numbers are given as percents (%). *Percent* literally means "per hundred." For example, 28% means 28 out of 100. What if there are about 14,000 trees in the forest and 28% are over 50 years old? How many of them are over 50 years old? Use your calculator. You want to find 28% of 14,000. Press [1][4][0][0][0] [×] [2][8][%]. The answer should be 3,920.

Mathematical Operations

Addition and subtraction are reverse operations, or inverses of each other. For example:

$2 + 3 = 5;$
$5 - 3 = 2;$
$5 - 2 = 3.$

Similarly, multiplication and division are also inverses of each other. For example:

$6 \times 3 = 18;$
$18 \div 6 = 3;$
$18 \div 3 = 6.$

Mathematical Statements

Mathematical statements using symbols may be true only when the symbols are replaced by certain numbers. For example:

$A < B$

If $A = 2$ and $B = 3$, the statement is true.
If $A = 3$ and $B = 2$, the statement is false.

Use Computers

A computer has many uses. The Internet connects your computer to many other computers around the world, so you can collect all kinds of information. You can use a computer to show this information and write reports. Best of all you can use a computer to explore, discover, and learn.

You can also get information from CD-ROMs. They are computer disks that can hold large amounts of information. You can fit a whole encyclopedia on one CD-ROM.

Use Computers for a Project

Here is how one group of students uses computers as they work on a weather project.

1. The students use instruments to measure temperature, wind speed, wind direction, and other parts of the weather. They input this information, or data, into the computer. The students keep the data in a table. This helps them compare the data from one day to the next.

Use Technology

2. The teacher finds out that another group of students in a town 200 kilometers to the west is also doing a weather project. The two groups use the Internet to talk to each other and share data. When a storm happens in the town to the west, that group tells the other group that it's coming their way.

3. The students want to find out more. They decide to stay on the Internet and send questions to a local TV weather forecaster. She has a Web site and answers questions from students every day.

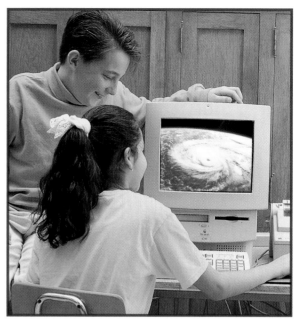

4. Meanwhile some students go to the library to gather more information from a CD-ROM. The CD-ROM has an encyclopedia that includes movie clips. The clips give examples of different kinds of storms.

5. The students have kept all their information in a folder called Weather Project. Now they use that information to write a report about the weather. On the computer they can move around paragraphs, add words, take out words, put in diagrams, and draw weather maps. Then they print the report in color.

Make Graphs to Organize Data

When you do an experiment in science, you collect information. To find out what your information means, you can organize it into graphs. There are many kinds of graphs.

Bar Graphs

A bar graph uses bars to show information. For example, what if you do an experiment by wrapping wire around a nail and connecting the ends of the wire to a battery? The nail then becomes a magnet that can pick up paper clips. The graph shows that the more you wrap the wire around the nail, the more paper clips it picks up. How many paper clips did the nail with 20 coils pick up? With 50 coils?

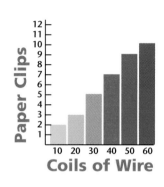

Pictographs

A pictograph uses symbols, or pictures, to show information. What if you collect information about how much water your family uses each day? The table shows what you find.

You can organize this information into the pictograph shown here. The pictograph has to explain what the symbol on the graph means. In this case each bottle means 20 liters of water. A half bottle means half of 20, or 10 liters of water.

1. Which activity uses the most water?
2. Which activity uses the least water?

Activity	Water Used Each Day (L)
Drinking	10
Showering	180
Bathing	240
Brushing teeth	80
Washing dishes	140
Washing hands	30
Washing clothes	280
Flushing toilet	90

A Family's Daily Use of Water

Drinking	
Showering	
Bathing	
Brushing teeth	
Washing dishes	
Washing hands	
Washing clothes	
Flushing toilet	

= 20 liters of water

Represent Data

Circle Graphs

A circle graph is helpful to show how a complete set of data is divided into parts. The circle graph here shows how water is used in the United States. What is the single largest use of water?

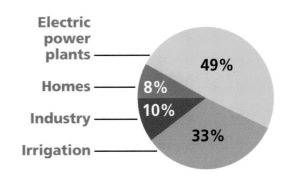

Electric power plants — 49%
Homes — 8%
Industry — 10%
Irrigation — 33%

Line Graphs

A line graph shows information by connecting dots plotted on the graph. It shows change over time. For example, what if you measure the temperature out of doors every hour starting at 6 A.M.? The table shows what you find.

Time	Temperature (°C)
6 A.M.	10
7 A.M.	12
8 A.M.	14
9 A.M.	16
10 A.M.	18
11 A.M.	20

You can organize this information into a line graph. Follow these steps.

1. Make a scale along the bottom and side of the graph. The scales should include all the numbers in the chart. Label the scales.
2. Plot points on the graph. For example, place your finger at the "6 A.M." on the bottom line. Place a finger from your other hand on the "10" on the left line. Move your "6 A.M." finger up and your "10" finger to the right until they meet, and make a pencil point. Plot the other points in this way.
3. Connect the points with a line.

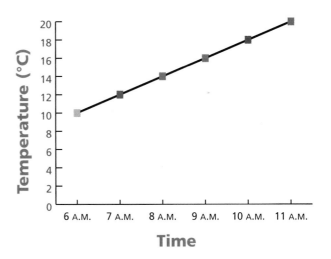

The line graph to the right organizes measurements you collected so that you can easily compare them.

1. Between which two weeks did the plant grow most?
2. When did plant growth begin to level off?

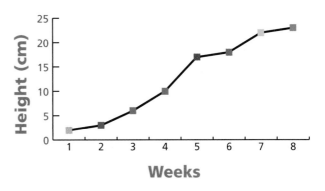

R 17

Make Maps to Show Information

Locate Places

A map is a drawing that shows an area from above. Most maps have coordinates—numbers and letters along the top and side. Coordinates help you find places easily. For example, what if you wanted to find the library on the map? It is located at B4. Place a finger on the letter B along the side of the map, and another finger on the number 4 at the top. Then move your fingers straight across and down the map until they meet. The library is located where the coordinates B and 4 meet, or very nearby.

1. What color building is located at F6?
2. The hospital is located three blocks north and two blocks east of the library. What are its coordinates?
3. Make a map of an area in your community. It might be a park or the area between your home and school. Include coordinates. Use a compass to find north, and mark north on your map. Exchange maps with class-mates, and answer each other's questions.

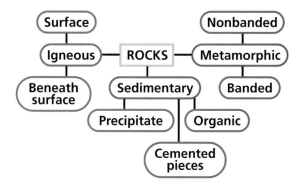

Idea Maps

The map below shows how places are connected to each other. Idea maps, on the other hand, show how ideas are connected to each other. Idea maps help you organize information about a topic.

The idea map above connects ideas about rocks. This map shows that there are three major types of rock—igneous, sedimentary, and metamorphic. Connections to each rock type provide further information. For example, this map reminds you that igneous rocks are classified into those that form at Earth's surface and far beneath it.

Make an idea map about a topic you are learning in science. Your map can include words, phrases, or even sentences. Arrange your map in a way that makes sense to you and helps you understand the ideas.

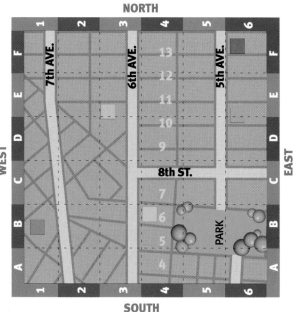

Represent Data

Make Tables and Charts to Organize Information

Tables help you organize data during experiments. Most tables have columns that run up and down, and rows that run across. The columns and rows have headings that tell you what kind of data goes in each part of the table.

A Sample Table

What if you are going to do an experiment to find out how long different kinds of seeds take to sprout? Before you begin the experiment, you should set up your table. Follow these steps.

1. In this experiment you will plant 20 radish seeds, 20 bean seeds, and 20 corn seeds. Your table must show how many radish seeds, bean seeds, and corn seeds sprouted on days 1, 2, 3, 4, and 5.

2. Make your table with columns, rows, and headings. You might use a computer to make a table. Some computer programs let you build a table with just the click of a mouse. You can delete or add columns and rows if you need to.

3. Give your table a title. Your table could look like the one here.

Make a Table

Now what if you are going to do an experiment to find out how temperature affects the sprouting of seeds? You will plant 20 bean seeds in each of two trays. You will keep each tray at a different temperature, as shown below, and observe the trays for seven days. Make a table you can use for this experiment.

Make a Chart

A chart is simply a table with pictures as well as words to label the rows or columns.

The Human Body

Like all organisms, humans are made up of cells. In fact, the human body is made of trillions of cells. These cells are organized into tissues, a group of similar cells that perform a specific function. Tissues, in turn, form organs. Your heart and lungs are examples of organs. Finally, organs work together as part of organ systems. Your heart, for example, is part of the circulatory system.

Levels of Organization

- Cells
- Tissues
- Organs
- Organ Systems
- Organism

Including the skin, or integumentary system, the human body has 11 major organ systems. These body systems each have specific functions, and they also work together as parts of the human body as a whole.

Human Body Systems	
System	**Function**
Nervous System	control
Skeletal System	support
Integumentary System	protection
Muscular System	movement
Circulatory System	transport
Respiratory System	oxygen/ carbon dioxide exchange
Digestive System	food absorption
Excretory System	waste removal
Endocrine System	regulation and control
Reproductive System	reproduction
Immune System	protection

The Nervous System

The nervous system has two parts. The brain and the spinal cord are the central nervous system. All other nerves are the outer, or peripheral, nervous system.

The largest part of the brain is the cerebrum. A deep groove separates the right half, or hemisphere, of the cerebrum from the left half. Both the right and left hemispheres of the cerebrum contain control centers for the senses.

The cerebellum lies below the cerebrum. It coordinates the skeletal muscles so they work smoothly together. It also helps in keeping balance.

The brain stem connects to the spinal cord. The lowest part of the brain stem is the medulla. It controls heartbeat, breathing, blood pressure, and the muscles in the digestive system.

Brain

Skull

Spinal cord

Nerves

Vertebral column

Spinal cord

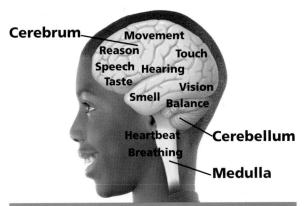

Cerebrum
- Movement
- Reason
- Touch
- Speech
- Hearing
- Taste
- Smell
- Vision
- Balance
- Heartbeat
- Breathing
- **Cerebellum**
- **Medulla**

Parts of a Neuron

The nerves in the nervous system are made up of nerve cells called *neurons.* Each neuron has three main parts—a cell body, dendrites, and an axon. Dendrites are branching nerve fibers that carry impulses, or electrical signals, toward the cell body. An axon is a nerve fiber that carries impulses away from the cell body.

When an impulse reaches the tip of an axon, it must cross a tiny gap to reach the next neuron. This gap between neurons is called a *synapse.*

CARE!

- **Wear protective headgear when you play sports or exercise.**

- **Stay away from drugs, such as stimulants, which can speed up the nervous system.**

- **Stay away from alcohol, which is a depressant and slows down the nervous system.**

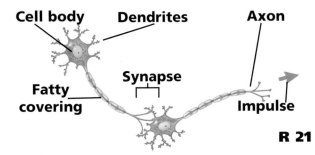

Cell body **Dendrites** **Axon**

Synapse

Fatty covering

Impulse

The Senses

Seeing

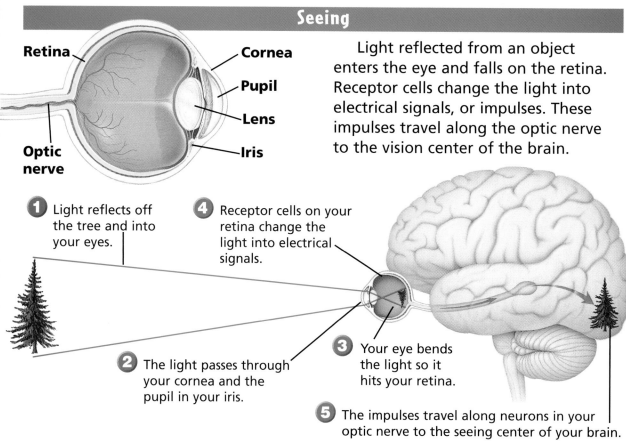

Retina

Cornea

Pupil

Lens

Iris

Optic nerve

Light reflected from an object enters the eye and falls on the retina. Receptor cells change the light into electrical signals, or impulses. These impulses travel along the optic nerve to the vision center of the brain.

1 Light reflects off the tree and into your eyes.

4 Receptor cells on your retina change the light into electrical signals.

2 The light passes through your cornea and the pupil in your iris.

3 Your eye bends the light so it hits your retina.

5 The impulses travel along neurons in your optic nerve to the seeing center of your brain.

Hearing

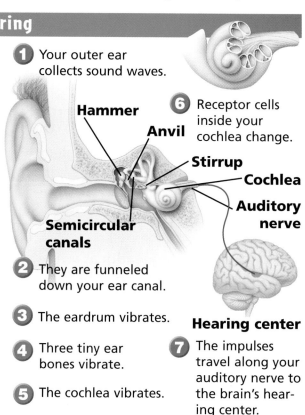

Sound waves enter the ear and cause the eardrum to vibrate. Receptor cells in the ear change the sound waves into impulses that travel along the auditory nerve to the hearing center of the brain.

1 Your outer ear collects sound waves.

6 Receptor cells inside your cochlea change.

Hammer

Anvil

Stirrup

Cochlea

Auditory nerve

Semicircular canals

CARE!

- To avoid straining your eye muscles, don't sit too close to the TV screen or computer monitor.

- Avoid loud music. Turn down the volume when wearing headphones.

2 They are funneled down your ear canal.

3 The eardrum vibrates.

4 Three tiny ear bones vibrate.

5 The cochlea vibrates.

Hearing center

7 The impulses travel along your auditory nerve to the brain's hearing center.

The Senses

Smelling

The sense of smell is really the ability to detect chemicals in the air. When a person breathes, chemicals dissolve in mucus in the upper part of the nose. When the chemicals come in contact with receptor cells, the cells send impulses along the olfactory nerve to the smelling center of the brain.

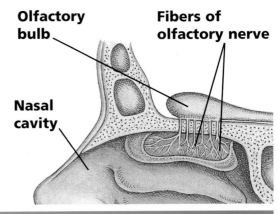

Olfactory bulb

Fibers of olfactory nerve

Nasal cavity

Tasting

When a person eats, chemicals in food dissolve in saliva. Saliva carries the chemicals to taste buds on the tongue. Inside each taste bud are receptors that can sense the four main tastes—sweet, sour, salty, and bitter. The receptors send impulses along a nerve to the taste center of the brain. The brain identifies the taste of the food, which is usually a combination of the four main tastes.

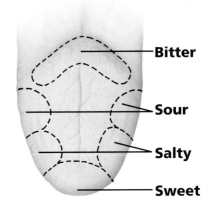

Bitter

Sour

Salty

Sweet

Touching

Receptor cells in the skin help a person tell hot from cold, wet from dry, and the light touch of a feather from the pressure of stepping on a stone. Each receptor cell sends impulses along sensory nerves to the spinal cord. The spinal cord then sends the impulses to the touch center of the brain.

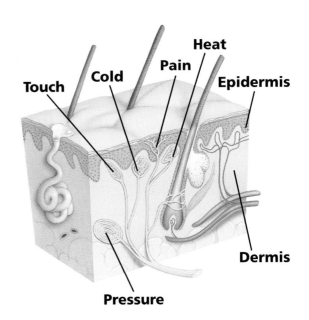

Touch **Cold** **Pain** **Heat** **Epidermis**

Dermis

Pressure

CARE!

- To prevent the spread of germs, always cover your mouth and nose when you cough or sneeze.

The Skeletal System

The body has a supporting frame, called a skeleton, which is made up of bones. The skeleton has several jobs.

- It gives the body its shape.
- It protects organs in the body.
- It works with muscles to move the body.

Each of the 206 bones of the skeleton is the size and shape best fitted to do its job. For example, long and strong leg bones support the body's weight.

CARE!

- Exercise to keep your skeletal system in good shape.
- Don't overextend your joints.
- Eat foods rich in vitamins and minerals. Your bones need the minerals, calcium, and phosphorus to grow strong.

The Integumentary System

The skeleton and the organ systems are covered by an outer layer of skin. The skin is the largest organ of the human body. It is part of the integumentary system. Other parts of the integumentary system are your hair, nails, and glands in the skin. The skin has several functions.

- It protects your internal organs.
- It protects your body from injury and infection.
- It helps regulate body temperature.
- It helps remove wastes.

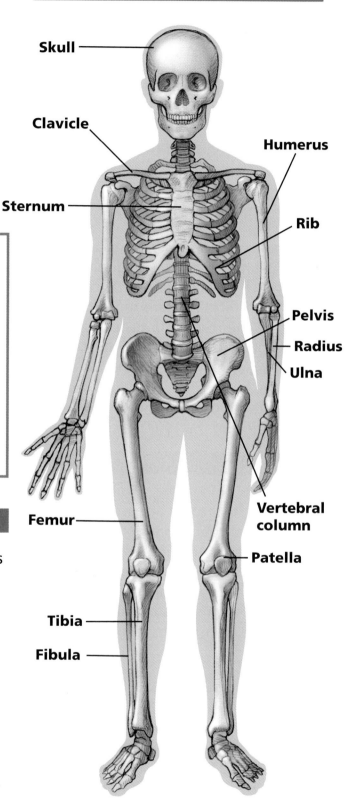

The Skeleton

- Skull
- Clavicle
- Sternum
- Humerus
- Rib
- Pelvis
- Radius
- Ulna
- Femur
- Vertebral column
- Patella
- Tibia
- Fibula

Joints

The skeleton has different types of joints. A joint is a place where two or more bones meet. Joints can be classified into three major groups—immovable joints, partly movable joints, and movable joints.

Types of Joints

Immovable Joints

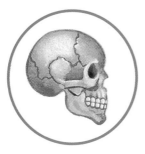

Head

Immovable joints are places where bones fit together too tightly to move. Nearly all the 29 bones in the skull meet at immovable joints. Only the lower jaw can move.

Partly Movable Joints

Partly movable joints are places where bones can move only a little. Ribs are connected to the sternum, or breastbone, with these joints.

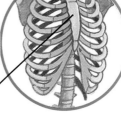

Ribs

Sternum

Movable Joints

Movable joints are places where bones can move easily.

Gliding joint

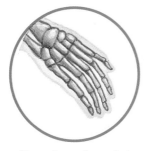

Hand and wrist

Small bones in the wrists and ankles meet at gliding joints. The bones can slide against one another. These joints allow some movement in all directions.

Ball-and-socket joint

The hips are examples of ball-and-socket joints. The ball of one bone fits into the socket, or cup, of another bone. These joints allow bones to move back and forth, in a circle, and side to side.

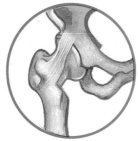

Hip

Hinge joint

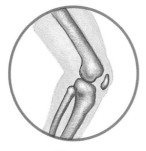

Knee

The knees are hinge joints. A hinge joint is similar to a door hinge. It allows bones to move back and forth in one direction.

Pivot joint

The joint between the skull and neck is a pivot joint. It allows the head to move up and down, and side to side.

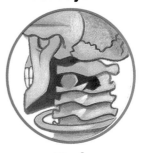

Neck

The Muscular System

Three types of muscles make up the body—skeletal muscle, cardiac muscle, and smooth muscle.

The muscles that are attached to and move bones are called *skeletal muscles.* These muscles are attached to bones by a tough cord called a *tendon.* Skeletal muscles pull bones to move them. Muscles do not push bones.

Cardiac muscles are found in only one place in the body—the heart. The walls of the heart are made of strong cardiac muscles. When cardiac muscles contract, they squeeze blood out of the heart. When cardiac muscles relax, the heart fills with more blood.

Smooth muscles make up internal organs and blood vessels. Smooth muscles in the lungs help a person breathe. Those in the blood vessels help control blood flow around the body.

CARE!

- **Exercise to strengthen your muscles.**
- **Eat the right foods.**
- **Get plenty of rest.**
- **Never take steroids unless your doctor tells you to.**

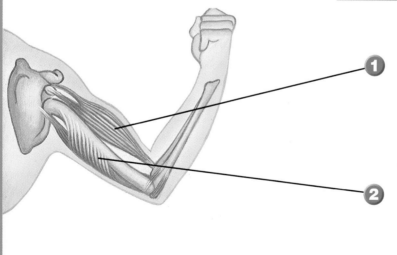

1 A message from you brain causes this muscle, called the biceps (BIGH·seps), to contract. When a muscle contracts, it becomes shorter and thicker. As the biceps contacts, it pulls on the arm bone it is attached to.

2 Most muscles work in pairs to move bones. This muscle, called the triceps (TRIGH·seps), relaxes when the biceps contacts. When a muscle relaxes, it becomes longer and thinner.

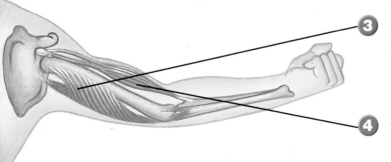

3 To straighten your arm, a message from your brain causes the triceps to contract. When the triceps contracts, it pulls on the bone it is attached to.

4 As the triceps contracts, the biceps relaxes. Your arm straightens.

Stimulus and Response

The nervous system, the skeletal system, and the muscular system work together to help you adjust to your surroundings. Anything in the environment that requires your body to adjust is called a *stimulus* (plural: stimuli). A reaction to a stimulus is called a *response*.

As you learned, nerve cells are called *neurons.* There are three kinds of neurons: sensory, associative, and motor. Each kind does a different job to help your body respond to stimuli.

- The job of your sensory neurons is to collect information from stimuli and send it to your brain and spinal cord. When you touch a sharp tack, sensory neurons alert your brain. The sensory neurons carry the message that your finger has touched a tack (stimulus) to the associative neurons in the brain and spinal cord.

- Associative neurons pass impulses from sensory to motor neurons. The message is interpreted and sent to the motor neurons.

- Motor neurons carry impulses from your brain and spinal cord to your muscles. The motor neurons cause your finger to move away from the tack (response).

In addition to responding to external stimuli, your body also responds to internal changes. Your body regulates its internal environment to maintain a stable condition for survival. This is called a *steady-state* condition.

Nerve Response

Nerves respond to a sharp object.

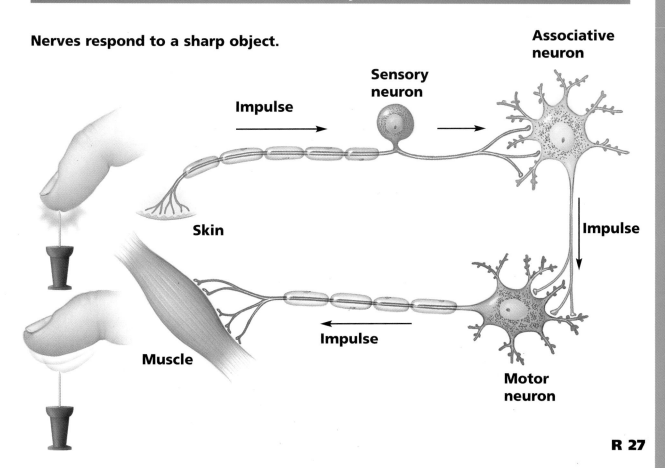

The Circulatory System

The circulatory system consists of the heart, blood vessels, and blood. Circulation is the flow of blood through the body. Blood is a liquid that contains red blood cells, white blood cells, and platelets. Red blood cells carry oxygen and nutrients to cells. White blood cells work to fight germs that enter the body. Platelets are cell fragments that make the blood clot.

The heart is a muscular organ about the size of a fist. It beats about 70 to 90 times a minute, pumping blood through the blood vessels. Arteries carry blood away from the heart. Some arteries carry blood to the lungs, where the cells pick up oxygen. Other arteries carry oxygen-rich blood from the lungs to all other parts of the body. Veins carry blood from other parts of the body back to the heart. Blood in most veins carries the wastes released by cells and has little oxygen. Blood flows from arteries to veins through narrow vessels called capillaries.

Pulse Rate and Pulse Points

You can tell how fast your heart is beating by checking your *pulse rate*. Take your pulse by putting the first and second fingers of one hand on the inside of the wrist of the other hand, just below the thumb. What you feel is the blood being pumped by your heart through arteries that lie close to the surface of the skin. Count the number of times you feel your heart pump in one minute. This is your pulse rate.

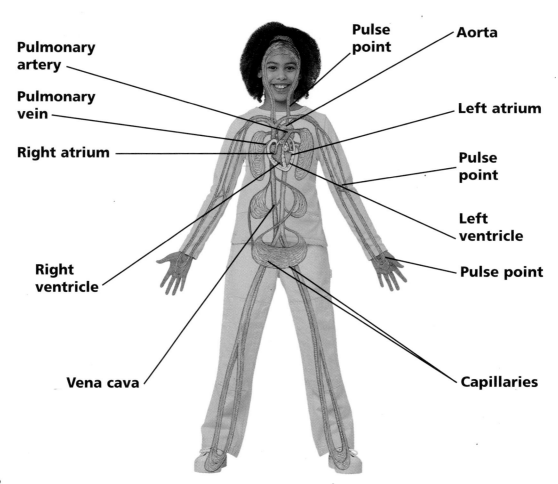

Pulmonary artery

Pulmonary vein

Right atrium

Right ventricle

Vena cava

Pulse point

Aorta

Left atrium

Pulse point

Left ventricle

Pulse point

Capillaries

The Heart

The heart has two sides, right and left, separated by a thick muscular wall. Each side has two chambers for blood. The upper chamber is the atrium. The lower chamber is the ventricle. Blood enters the heart through the vena cava. It leaves the heart through the aorta.

The pulmonary artery carries blood from the body into the lungs. Here carbon dioxide leaves the blood to be exhaled by the lungs. Fresh oxygen enters the blood to be carried to every cell in the body. Blood returns from the lungs to the heart through the pulmonary veins.

CARE!

- Don't smoke. The nicotine in tobacco makes the heart beat faster and work harder to pump blood.

- Never take illegal drugs, such as cocaine or heroin. They can damage the heart and cause heart failure.

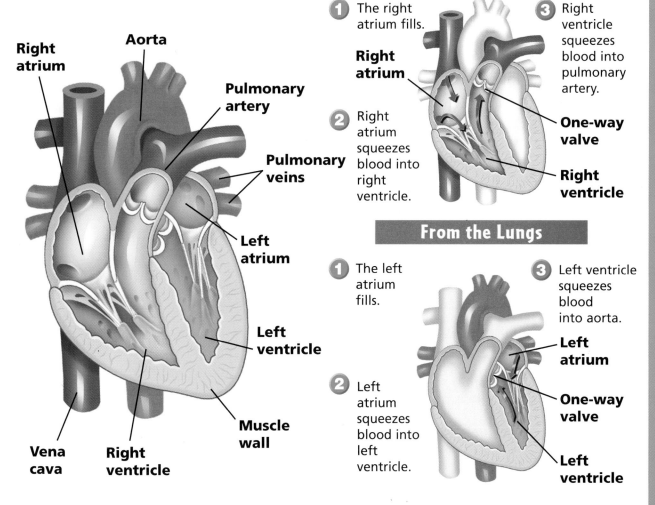

How the Heart Works

Right atrium

Aorta

Pulmonary artery

Pulmonary veins

Left atrium

Left ventricle

Muscle wall

Vena cava

Right ventricle

To the Lungs

1 The right atrium fills.

Right atrium

2 Right atrium squeezes blood into right ventricle.

3 Right ventricle squeezes blood into pulmonary artery.

One-way valve

Right ventricle

From the Lungs

1 The left atrium fills.

2 Left atrium squeezes blood into left ventricle.

3 Left ventricle squeezes blood into aorta.

Left atrium

One-way valve

Left ventricle

The Respiratory System

The process of getting and using oxygen in the body is called respiration. When a person inhales, air is pulled into the nose or mouth. The air travels down into the trachea. In the chest the trachea divides into two bronchial tubes. One bronchial tube enters each lung. Each bronchial tube branches into smaller tubes called bronchioles.

At the end of each bronchiole are tiny air sacs called alveoli. The alveoli exchange carbon dioxide for oxygen.

Oxygen comes from the air a person breathes. Two main muscles control breathing. One is located between the ribs. The other is a dome-shaped sheet of muscle called the diaphragm.

To inhale, the diaphragm contracts and pulls down. Other muscles pull the ribs up and out. This makes more room in the chest. Air rushes into the lungs and fills the space.

To exhale, the diaphragm relaxes and returns to its dome shape. The lungs get smaller and force the air out.

CARE!

- **Don't smoke. Smoking damages your respiratory system.**

- **Exercise to strengthen your breathing muscles.**

- **If you ever have trouble breathing, tell an adult at once.**

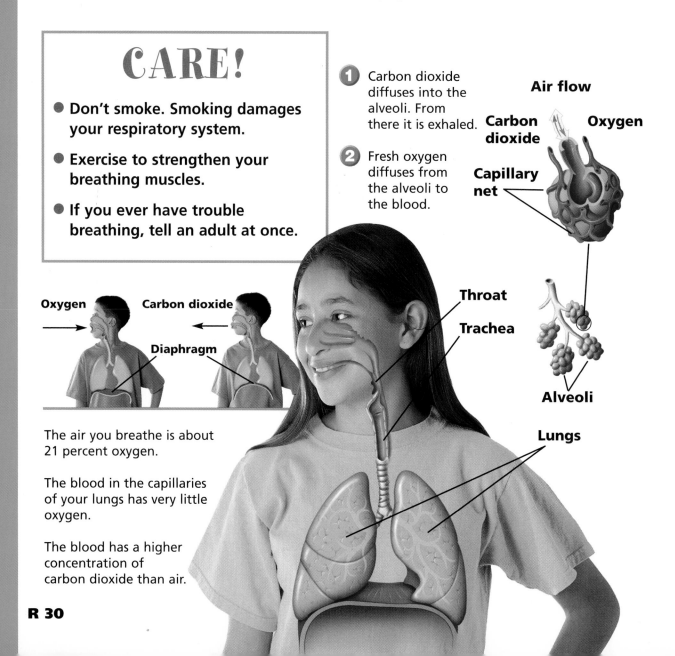

1 Carbon dioxide diffuses into the alveoli. From there it is exhaled.

2 Fresh oxygen diffuses from the alveoli to the blood.

Air flow

Carbon dioxide **Oxygen**

Capillary net

Throat

Trachea

Alveoli

Lungs

Oxygen Carbon dioxide

Diaphragm

The air you breathe is about 21 percent oxygen.

The blood in the capillaries of your lungs has very little oxygen.

The blood has a higher concentration of carbon dioxide than air.

Effects of Exercise

Any type of exercise uses your muscles. When you exercise, your muscles need three things:

- They need oxygen.
- They need to remove wastes.
- They need to get rid of heat.

When you exercise, several things happen to your body. Your heart beats faster, you breathe heavier and faster, and you sweat.

If you are going to be exercising for more than a couple of minutes, your body needs to get oxygen to the muscles or the muscles will stop working. Your body increases the flow of oxygen-rich blood to working muscle as follows:

- Your rate and depth of breathing increase to take in more oxygen.
- Your heart beats faster so that it can pump more oxygen-rich blood to the muscles.

Sweating helps remove both wastes and heat that result from exercise.

The Digestive System

Digestion is the process of breaking down food into simple substances the body can use. Digestion begins when a person chews food. Chewing breaks the food down into smaller pieces and moistens it with saliva. Saliva is produced by the salivary glands.

Digested food is absorbed in the small intestine. The walls of the small intestine are lined with villi. Villi are tiny fingerlike projections that absorb digested food. From the villi the blood transports nutrients to every part of the body.

The shape of the small intestine's villi increases the amount of nutrients that can be absorbed from the food.

CARE!

● Chew your food well.

● Drink plenty of water to help move food through your digestive system.

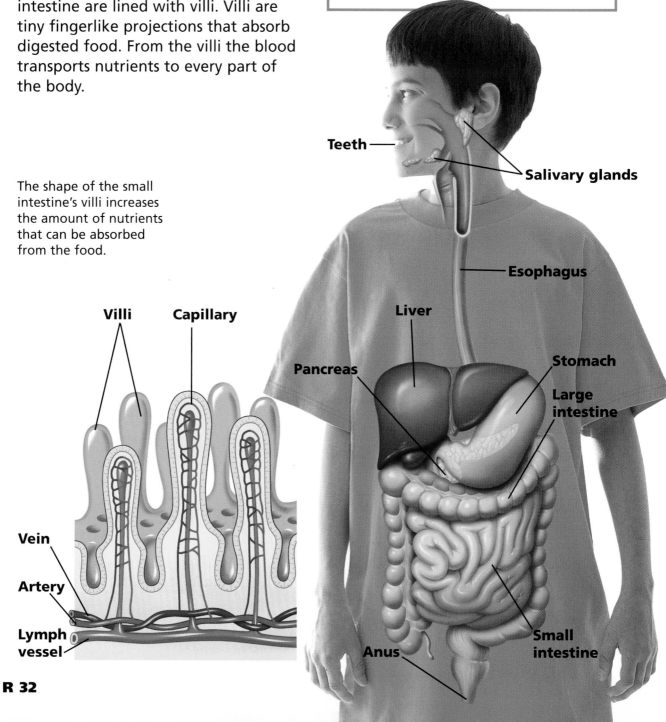

Teeth

Salivary glands

Esophagus

Liver

Villi

Capillary

Pancreas

Stomach

Large intestine

Vein

Artery

Lymph vessel

Anus

Small intestine

The Digestive System

Mechanical and Chemical Digestion

Digestion is both mechanical and chemical. Chewing is the first step in digestion. Chewing is *mechanical digestion*, the physical process of breaking food down into smaller pieces. As you chew, saliva begins to break the food into simpler molecules. This is *chemical digestion*.

After you swallow your food, both mechanical and chemical digestion continue in the stomach. Stomach muscles churn food particles into smaller pieces. Glands lining the stomach produce strong digestive juices.

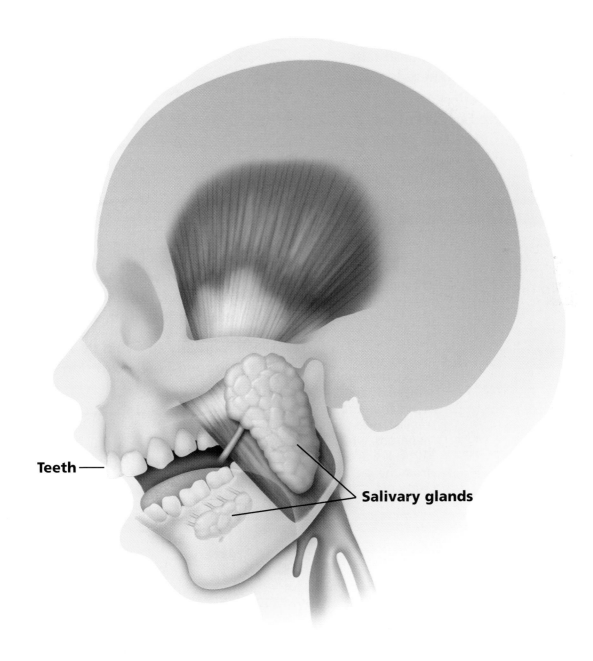

Teeth —

Salivary glands

The Excretory System

Excretion is the process of removing waste products from the body. The liver filters wastes from the blood and converts them into urea. Urea is then carried to the kidneys for excretion. Each kidney contains more than a million nephrons. Nephrons are structures in the kidneys that filter blood.

The skin takes part in excretion when a person sweats. Glands in the inner layer of the skin produce sweat. Sweat is mostly water. Sweat tastes salty because it contains mineral salts the body doesn't need. There is also a tiny amount of urea in sweat.

Sweat is excreted by the sweat glands onto the outer layer of the skin. There it evaporates into the air. Evaporation takes place in part because of body heat. When sweat evaporates, a person feels cooler. On hot days or when exercising, a person sweats more to keep the body from overheating.

How You Sweat

Glands under your skin push sweat up to the surface, where it collects.

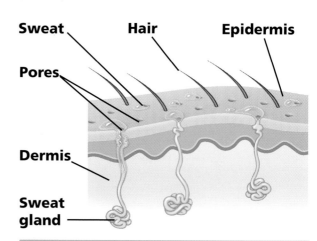

Sweat **Hair** **Epidermis**
Pores
Dermis
Sweat gland

How Your Kidneys Work

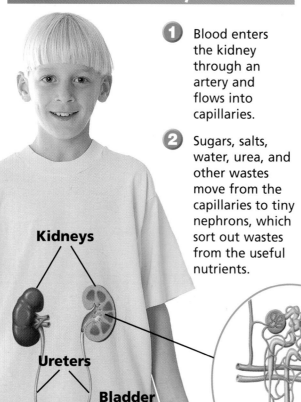

Kidneys

Ureters

Bladder

Urethra

1. Blood enters the kidney through an artery and flows into capillaries.

2. Sugars, salts, water, urea, and other wastes move from the capillaries to tiny nephrons, which sort out wastes from the useful nutrients.

CARE!

- Drink plenty of water to help the kidneys do their job and to replace water loss from sweating.

- Wash regularly to avoid body odor, clogged pores, and skin irritation.

3. The nutrients return to the blood and flow back out through veins.

4. Urea and other wastes become urine, which flows down the ureters.

5. Urine is stored in the bladder and excreted through the urethra.

Artery

Vein

Capillaries

The Excretory System

Removing Excess Heat

In addition to waste removal, one of the skin's most important jobs is to maintain internal body temperature. The skin does this by removing excess heat. Two things happen when you exercise: your face gets red and you sweat. Both are ways of getting rid of excess heat.

The nervous system, the circulatory system, and the skin all work together to regulate body temperature. The diagram below shows what happens when your body heats up as a result of exercise.

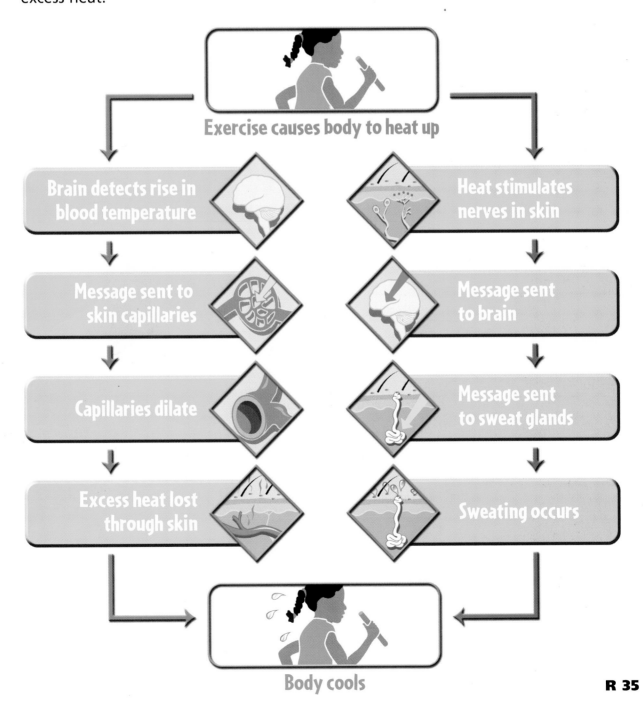

Exercise causes body to heat up

Brain detects rise in blood temperature

Heat stimulates nerves in skin

Message sent to skin capillaries

Message sent to brain

Capillaries dilate

Message sent to sweat glands

Excess heat lost through skin

Sweating occurs

Body cools

The Endocrine System

Hormones are chemicals that control body functions. A gland that produces hormones is called an endocrine gland. Sweat from sweat glands flows out of tubes called ducts. Endocrine glands have no ducts.

The endocrine glands are scattered around the body. Each gland makes one or more hormones. Every hormone seeks out a target organ, the place in the body where the hormone acts.

The endocrine glands help to maintain a *steady-state* condition in your body. They can turn the production of hormones on or off when they sense that too little or too much is being produced.

CARE!

● Doctors can treat many diseases, such as diabetes, caused by endocrine glands that produce too little or too much of a hormone.

Some Glands in the Endocrine System

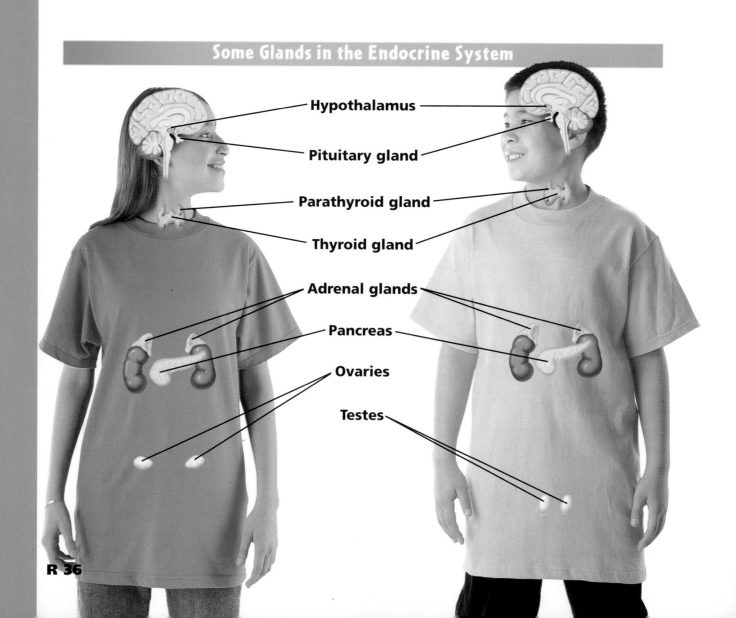

Hypothalamus

Pituitary gland

Parathyroid gland

Thyroid gland

Adrenal glands

Pancreas

Ovaries

Testes

The Reproductive System

The testes are the male reproductive organs. At puberty the testes begin to produce sperm. Sperm move through sperm ducts, where they mix with fluid from endocrine glands.

The ovaries are the female reproductive organs, which contain eggs. After puberty one mature egg is released about once every 28 days. The egg moves to the oviduct, a narrow tube leading from the ovary.

CARE!

- **Abstinence is the only sure way to avoid sexually transmitted diseases.**

The Male Reproductive System

Sperm move from the testes through sperm ducts, where they mix with fluid from the glands. The sperm and fluid move through the urethra.

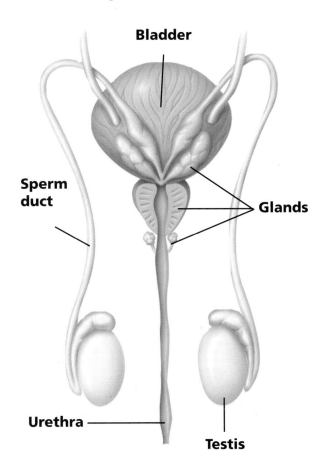

Bladder

Sperm duct

Glands

Urethra

Testis

The Female Reproductive System

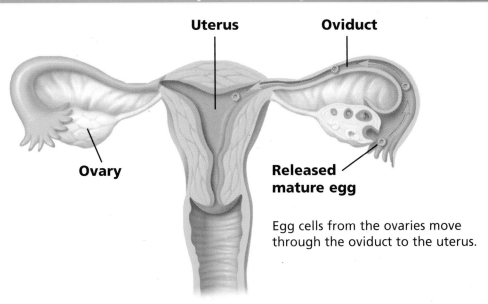

Uterus

Oviduct

Ovary

Released mature egg

Egg cells from the ovaries move through the oviduct to the uterus.

R 37

The Immune System

The immune system helps the body fight disease. Inside some bones is a soft tissue known as red marrow that fills the spaces in spongy bone. Red marrow makes new red blood cells, platelets that stop a cut from bleeding, and germ-fighting white blood cells.

There are white blood cells in the blood vessels and in the lymph vessels. Lymph vessels are similar to blood vessels. Instead of blood, they carry lymph. Lymph is a straw-colored fluid surrounding body cells.

Lymph nodes filter out harmful materials in lymph. Like red marrow, they also produce white blood cells to fight infections. Swollen lymph nodes in the neck are a clue that the body is fighting germs.

CARE!

- Be sure to get immunized against common diseases.

- Keep cuts clean to prevent infection.

1 A bone is covered with a tough but thin membrane that has many small blood vessels. The blood vessels bring nutrients and oxygen to the living parts of the bone and remove wastes.

2 Inside some bones is a soft tissue known as marrow. Yellow marrow is made mostly of fat cells and is one of the body's energy reserves. It is usually found in the long, hollow spaces of long bones.

3 Part of the bone is compact, or solid. It is made up of living bone cells and nonliving materials. The nonliving part is made up of layers of hardened minerals such as calcium and phosphorus. In between the mineral layers are living bone cells.

4 Red marrow fills the spaces in spongy bone. Red marrow makes new red blood cells, germ-fighting white blood cells, and platelets that stop a cut from bleeding.

5 Part of the bone is made of bone tissue that looks like a dry sponge. It is made of strong, hard tubes. It is also found in the middle of short, flat bones.

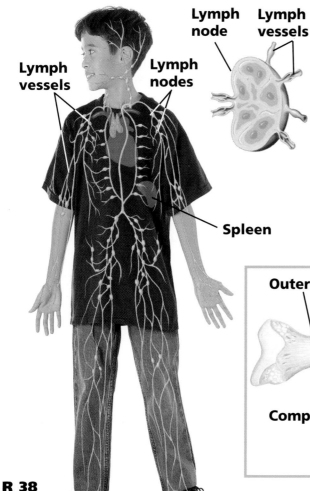

Lymph vessels

Lymph nodes

Lymph node

Lymph vessels

Spleen

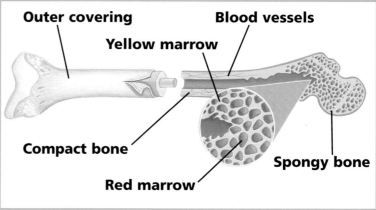

Outer covering

Yellow marrow

Blood vessels

Compact bone

Red marrow

Spongy bone

Infectious Diseases

A disease is anything that breaks down the normal functions of the body. Some diseases are inherited. Others are caused by harmful materials in the environment. Many diseases, however, are caused by organisms.

Disease-causing organisms include bacteria and viruses. Diseases caused by these organisms are called *infectious diseases* because the organisms enter, or infect, the body.

Human Infectious Diseases		
Disease	**Caused by**	**Organ System Affected**
Chicken pox	Virus	Skin
Smallpox	Virus	Skin
Polio	Virus	Nervous system
Rabies	Virus	Nervous system
Influenza	Virus	Respiratory system
Measles	Virus	Skin
Mumps	Virus	Salivary glands
Tuberculosis	Bacteria	Respiratory system
Tetanus	Bacteria	Nervous system
Food poisoning	Bacteria	Digestive system

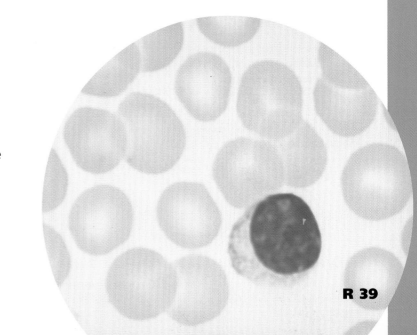

White blood cells are your body's main protection against infectious disease. The white blood cells leave the blood vessels or lymph vessels to fight disease organisms in your tissues.

Staying Healthy

Physical fitness is the condition in which the body is healthy and works the best it can. It involves working the skeletal muscles, bones, joints, heart, and respiratory system.

3–5 times a week Aerobic activities such as swimming; sports activities such as basketball, handball

Daily Substitute activity for inactivity—take the stairs, walk instead of riding

Occasionally
Inactive pastimes such as watching TV

2–3 times a week
Leisure activities such as gardening, golf, softball

Activity Pyramid

CARE!

- Stay active every day.
- Eat a balanced diet.
- Drink plenty of water—6 to 8 large glasses a day.

There is more to fitness than exercise. To make sure your body gets all the nutrients you need, you should eat a balanced diet. *A balanced diet* includes all the major food groups.

A balanced diet provides the calories, or energy from food, that you need to stay healthy. The number of calories needed varies from person to person, depending on their metabolism. *Metabolism* is the rate at which you burn energy. It is determined by weight, age, sex, and level of activity.

Fats, oils, and sweets
Use sparingly

Milk, yogurt, and cheese group
2–3 servings

Meat, poultry, fish, dry beans, eggs, and nuts group
2–3 servings

Vegetable group
3–5 servings

Fruit group
2–4 servings

Bread, cereal, rice, and pasta group
6–11 servings

Food Guide Pyramid

FOLDABLES™

by Dinah Zike

Folding Instructions

So how do you make a Foldables data organizer? The following pages offer step-by-step instructions—where and when to fold, where to cut—for making 11 basic Foldables data organizers. The instructions begin with the basic shapes, such as the hot dog fold, that were introduced on page xv.

Half-Book

Fold a sheet of paper ($8\frac{1}{2}$" x 11") in half.

1. This book can be folded vertically like a hot dog or …

2. … it can be folded horizontally like a hamburger.

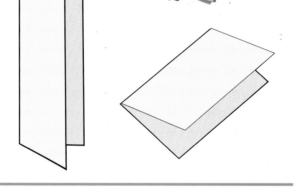

Folded Book

1. Make a Half-Book.

2. Fold in half again like a hamburger.

This makes a ready-made cover and two small pages inside for recording information.

Two-Tab Book

Take a Folded Book and cut up the valley of the inside fold toward the mountain top.

This cut forms two large tabs that can be used front and back for writing and illustrations.

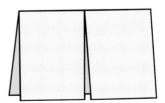

Pocket Book

1. Fold a sheet of paper ($8\frac{1}{2}$" x 11") in half like a hamburger.

2. Open the folded paper and fold one of the long sides up two inches to form a pocket. Refold along the hamburger fold so that the newly formed pockets are on the inside.

3. Glue the outer edges of the two-inch fold with a small amount of glue.

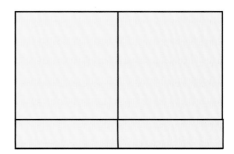

Shutter Fold

1. Begin as if you were going to make a hamburger, but instead of creasing the paper, pinch it to show the midpoint.

2. Fold the outer edges of the paper to meet at the pinch, or midpoint, forming a Shutter Fold.

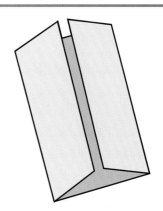

Trifold Book

1. Fold a sheet of paper ($8\frac{1}{2}$" x 11") into thirds.

2. Use this book as is, or cut into shapes.

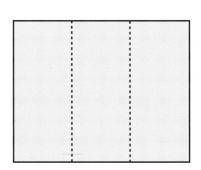

Three-Tab Book

1. Fold a sheet of paper like a hot dog.

2. With the paper horizontal and the fold of the hot dog up, fold the right side toward the center, trying to cover one half of the paper.

3. Fold the left side over the right side to make a book with three folds.

4. Open the folded book. Place one hand between the two thicknesses of paper and cut up the two valleys on one side only. This will create three tabs.

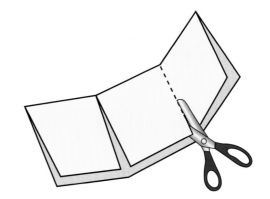

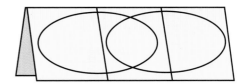

Layered-Look Book

1. Stack two sheets of paper ($8\frac{1}{2}$" x 11") so that the back sheet is one inch higher than the front sheet.

2. Bring the bottoms of both sheets upward and align the edges so that all of the layers or tabs are the same distance apart.

3. When all the tabs are an equal distance apart, fold the papers and crease well.

4. Open the papers and glue them together along the valley, or inner center fold, or staple them along the mountain.

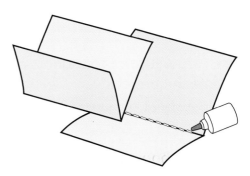

Four-Tab Book

1. Fold a sheet of paper ($8\frac{1}{2}$" x 11") in half like a hot dog.

2. Fold this long rectangle in half like a hamburger.

3. Fold both ends back to touch the mountain top or fold it like an accordion.

4. On the side with two valleys and one mountain top, make vertical cuts through one thickness of paper, forming four tabs.

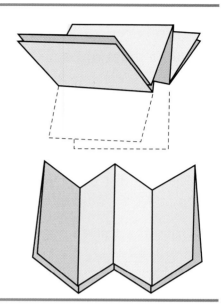

Four-Door Book

1. Make a Shutter Fold using 11" x 17" or 12" x 18" paper.

2. Fold the Shutter Fold in half like a hamburger. Crease well.

3. Open the project and cut along the two inside valley folds.

These cuts will form four doors on the inside of the project.

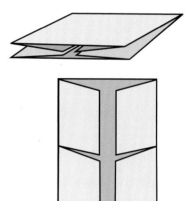

Folded Table or Chart

1. Fold the number of vertical columns needed to make the table or chart.

2. Fold the horizontal rows needed to make the table or chart.

3. Label the rows and columns.

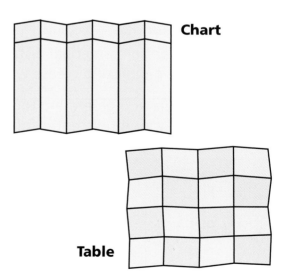

Chart

Table

Glossary

This Glossary will help you to pronounce and understand the meanings of the Science Words introduced in this book. The page number at the end of the definition tells where the word appears.

A

abiotic factor (ā′bī ot′ik fak′tər) A nonliving part of an ecosystem. (p. B6)

absorption (əb sôrp′shən) The disappearance of a sound wave into a surface. (p. F66)

abyssal plain (ə bis′əl plān) The vast flat lands beyond the continental shelf that cover almost half of the deep ocean floor. (p. C90)

acceleration (ak sel′ə rā′shən) Change in velocity with respect to time. (pp. F13, F22)

acid (as′id) A substance that tastes sour and turns blue litmus paper red. (p. E82)

acid rain (as′id rān) Moisture that falls to Earth after being mixed with wastes from burned fossil fuels. (p. C65)

acidity (ə sid′ə tē) The strength of an acid. (p. E86)

action (ak′shən) The force one object applies to a second, as in Newton's third law of motion, which states, "For every action, there is an equal but opposite reaction." *See* **reaction**. (p. F24)

adaptation (ad′əp tā′shən) A characteristic that enables a living thing to survive in its environment. (pp. A46, A106)

aerial root (âr′ē əl rüt) A root that never touches the ground but can take in moisture from the air. (p. A31)

aerosol (âr′ə sōl′) A type of colloid in which liquid drops or solid particles are spread throughout a gas. (p. E60)

air mass (âr mas) A large region of the atmosphere where the air has similar properties throughout. (p. D70)

air pressure (âr presh′ər) The force put on a given area by the weight of the air above it. (p. D33)

alkalinity (al′kə lin′i tē) The strength of a base. (p. E86)

alternative energy source (ōl tûr′nə tiv en′ər jē sôrs) A source of energy other than the burning of a fossil fuel. (p. C104)

amphibian (am fib′ē ən) A vertebrate that lives part of its life in water and part of its life on land. (p. A95)

anemometer (an′ə mom′i tər) A device that measures wind speed. (p. D64)

PRONUNCIATION KEY

The following symbols are used throughout the McGraw-Hill Science Glossaries.

a	at	e	end	o	hot	u	up	hw	white	ə	about
ā	ape	ē	me	ō	old	ū	use	ng	song		taken
ä	far	i	it	ôr	fork	ü	rule	th	thin		pencil
âr	care	ī	ice	oi	oil	ů	pull	th	this		lemon
ô	law	îr	pierce	ou	out	ûr	turn	zh	measure		circus

′ = primary accent; shows which syllable takes the main stress, such as **kil** in **kilogram** (kil′ə gram′).

′ = secondary accent; shows which syllables take lighter stresses, such as **gram** in **kilogram**.

aneroid barometer (an'ə roid bə rom'i tər) A spring enclosed in a pleated metal can that expands or contracts to indicate changes in air pressure. (p. D34)

angiosperm (an'jē ə spûrm') A seed plant that produces flowers. *See* **gymnosperm**. (p. A68)

aquifer (ak'wə fər) An underground layer of rock or soil filled with water. (p. C75)

asexual reproduction (a sek'shü əl rē'prō duk'shən) The production of a new organism from only one cell. (p. A62)

asteroid (as'tə roid') "Minor planet." One of many small, rocky objects that orbit the Sun between the orbits of Mars and Jupiter. (p. D19)

asteroid belt (as'tə roid' belt) Region between Mars and Jupiter where most asteroids are found. (p. D19)

atmosphere (at'məs fîr') The blanket of gases that surrounds Earth. (pp. C26, D32)

atom (at'əm) The smallest unit of an element that retains the properties of that element. *See* **molecule**. (p. E26)

aurora (ə rôr'ə) The northern or southern lights that appear in the night sky, especially in polar regions. (p. D32)

B

bacterium (bak tîr'ē əm) *sing., n. pl.* **bacteria** (-ē ə) A member of either of two kingdoms of one-celled living things that have no nucleus, or center, in their cell body. (p. A19)

balanced forces (bal'ənst fôrs'əz) Forces that cancel each other out when acting together on a single object. (p. F21)

barometer (bə rom'i tər) A device for measuring air pressure. (p. D34)

base (bās) A substance that tastes bitter and turns red litmus paper blue. (p. E82)

basin (bās'in) The floor of an ocean, containing mountains, valleys, and plains. (p. C84)

bench mark (bench' märk') A plaque left by surveyors to tell the exact location and elevation of a place. (p. C6)

benthos (ben'thos) Organisms that live on the bottom in aquatic ecosystems. (p. B72)

bird (bûrd) A vertebrate that has both feathers and wings. (p. C95)

biomass (bī'ō mas') Energy from plant matter or animal waste. (p. C106)

biome (bī'ōm) One of Earth's large ecosystems, with its own kind of climate, soil, plants, and animals. (p. B64)

biotic factor (bī ot'ik fak'tər) A living part of an ecosystem. (p. B7)

boiling point (boil'ing point) The particular temperature for each substance at which it changes state from a liquid to a gas. (p. E37)

buoyancy (boi'ən sē) The upward push of a liquid on an object placed in it. (p. E12)

C

cambium (kam'bē əm) The layer in plants that separates the xylem from the phloem. (p. A31, A32)

camouflage (kam'ə fläzh') An adaptation in which an animal protects itself against predators by blending in with the environment. (p. A108)

carbon cycle (kär'bən sī'kəl) The continuous exchange of carbon dioxide and oxygen among living things. (p. B53)

carnivore (kär'nə vôr') An animal that eats another animal. (p. B20)

carrying capacity (kar'ē ing kə pas'i tē) The maximum population size that an area can support. (p. B35)

cell (sel) The smallest unit of living matter. (p. A6)

chemical change (kem'i kəl chānj) A change of matter that occurs when atoms link together in a new way, creating a new substance different from the original substances. (p. E71)

chemical formula (kəm'i kəl fôr'myə lə) A way to write a compound's name using symbols. The letters tell what elements are in the compound, and the subscripts tell the number of particles in the compound. (p. E25)

chemical reaction (kem'i kəl rē ak'shən) Another name for chemical change. (p. E71)

chemosynthesis (kē'mō sin'thə sis) In tube worms the process by which bacteria create nutrients from hydrogen sulfide and oxygen, using chemical reactions rather than light. (p. C93)

chlorophyll (klôr'ə fil') A green chemical in plant cells that allows plants to use the Sun's energy for making food. (p. A6)

cirrus cloud (sir'əs kloud) A high-altitude cloud with a featherlike shape, made of ice crystals. (p. D44)

classification (klas'ə fi kā'shən) The science of finding patterns among living things. (p. A10)

cleavage (klē'vij) The tendency of a mineral to break along flat surfaces. (p. C34)

climate (klī'mit) The average weather pattern of a region. (p. D84)

climate zone (klī mat' zōn) A region that has similar weather patterns based on temperature, precipitation, wind, distance from a coast, mountain ranges, ocean currents, and vegetation. (p. D84)

climax community (klī'maks kə mū'ni tē) The final stage of succession in an area, unless a major change happens. (p. B84)

cold front (kōld frunt) A front where cold air moves in under a warm air mass. (p. D72)

colloid (kol'oid) A special type of mixture in which the particles of one material are scattered through another and block the passage of light without settling out. (pp. E54, E60)

comet (kom' it) A "dirty snowball" orbiting the Sun — a mixture of ices, frozen gases, rock, and dust left over from the formation of the solar system. (p. D19)

commensalism (kə men'sə liz'əm) A relationship between two kinds of organisms that benefits one without harming the other. (p. B27)

community (kə mū'ni tē) All the living things in an ecosystem. (p. B11)

complete flower (kəm plēt' flou'ər) A flower that has sepals, petals, stamens, and pistils. (p. A78)

compound (kom'pound) Any substance that is formed by the chemical combination of two or more elements and acts like a single substance. (p. E24)

compression (kəm presh'ən) **1.** The part of a sound wave where molecules are crowded together. (p. F51) **2.** A movement of plates that presses together or squeezes Earth's crust. (p. C8)

concave lens (kon kāv' lenz) A lens that is thicker at the edges than at the middle. As it curves inward, it spreads light rays apart, making images appear smaller. (p. F100)

concave mirror (kon kāv' mir'ər) A mirror that curves in on the shiny side. (p. F88)

condensation (kon'den sā'shən) *n.* The changing of a gas into a liquid. (pp. B50, D39) —**condense** (kən dens') *v.* (p. E37)

PRONUNCIATION KEY

a at; ā ape; ä far; âr care; ô law; e end; ē me; i it; ī ice; îr pierce; o hot; ō old; ôr fork; oi oil; ou out; u up; ū use; ü rule; ù pull; ûr turn; hw white; ng song; th thin; <u>th</u> this; zh measure; ə about, taken, pencil, lemon, circus

conduction (kən duk′shən) *n.* The passing of heat through a material while the material itself stays in place. (p. E97) **—conduct** (kən dukt′) *v.* (p. E14)

conifer (kon′ə fər) Any of a group of gymnosperms that produce seeds in cones and have needlelike leaves. (p. A69)

conserve (kən′sûrv′) To save, protect, or use resources wisely. (p. C39)

constellation (kon′stə lā′shən) Patterns formed by groups of stars in the night sky. (p. D12)

consumer (kən sü′mər) Any animal that eats plants or eats other plant-eating animals. (pp. B7, B20)

continental rise (kon′tə nen′təl rīz) A buildup of sediment on the sea floor at the bottom of the continental slope. It is a zone of sand and mud that stretches from the slope down to the deep-sea floor. (p. C90)

continental shelf (kon′tə nen′təl shelf) The underwater edge of a continent. (p. C90)

continental slope (kon′tə nen′təl slōp) The steep slope leading down from the continental shelf toward the sea floor. (p. C90)

contour plowing (kon′tür plou′ing) Preventing erosion by plowing across rather than up and down a slope. (p. C51)

contract (kən trakt′) To shrink, as when a material gets colder. (p. E41)

convection (kən vek′shən) The flow of heat through a liquid or a gas, causing hot parts to rise and cooler parts to sink. (p. E97)

convection cell (kən vek′shən sel) A circular pattern of air rising, air sinking, and wind. (p. D55)

convex lens (kon veks′ lenz) A lens that is thicker at the middle than at the edges. As it curves outward, it brings light together, making images appear larger. (p. F100)

convex mirror (kon veks′ mir′ər) A mirror that curves out on the shiny side. (p. F88)

coquina (kō kē′nə) A sedimentary rock formed from seashell fragments. (p. C44)

Coriolis effect (kôr′ē ō′lis i fekt′) The curving of the path of a moving object caused by Earth's rotation. (p. D57)

cortex (kôr′teks) The layer of tissue just inside the epidermis of a plant's roots and stems. (p. A30)

cotyledon (ko′tə lē′dən) A tiny leaflike structure, also called a seedleaf, inside the seed of an angiosperm. (p. A72)

crop rotation (krop rō tā′shən) Growing different crops each year so that the soil does not use up the same kinds of minerals year after year. (p. C51)

crossbreeding (krôs′brēd′ing) Producing offspring by mating individuals from two distinct breeds or varieties of the same species. (p. A112)

cross-pollination (krôs′pol′ə nā′shən) The transfer of pollen from one flower to another. (p. A80)

crust (krust) The rocky surface that makes up the top of the lithosphere and includes the continents and the ocean floor. (p. C7)

crystal (kris′təl) The geometric shape a mineral forms when its atoms and molecules get into fixed patterns. (p. C32)

cumulus cloud (kū′myə ləs kloud) A puffy cloud that appears to rise up from a flat bottom. (p. D44)

current (kûr′ənt) An ocean movement; a large stream of water that flows in the ocean. (p. C86)

cycad (sī′kad) One of the evergreen gymnosperms that resemble palms and have seed-bearing cones. (p. A69)

decibel (dB) (des′ə bel′) A unit that measures loudness. (p. F58)

deciduous (di sij′ü əs) Said of a plant that loses its leaves each fall. *See* **evergreen**. (pp. A69, B70)

deciduous forest (di si′jə wəs fôr′ist) A forest biome with many kinds of trees that lose their leaves each autumn. (p. B70)

decomposer (dē′kəm pōz′ər) Any of the fungi or bacteria that break down dead plants and animals into useful things like minerals and rich soil. (pp. B7, B21, B56)

delta (del′tə) Fan-shaped region formed by deposits of sediments found at the mouth of a river. (p. C21)

density (den′si tē) A measure of how tightly packed the matter in an object is. (pp. C35, E8)

deposition (dep′ə zish′ən) The dropping off of bits of eroded rock. (p. C13)

desalination (dē sal′ə nā′shən) Getting fresh water from seawater. (p. C73)

desert (dez′ərt) A sandy or rocky biome, with little precipitation and little plant life. (p. B69)

dicot (dī′kot′) An angiosperm with two cotyledons in each seed. *See* **monocot**. (p. A72)

dinoflagellate (din′ə flaj′ə lāt′) A protist containing chlorophyll that has two flagella for motion. When they overreproduce, they can cause "red tides." (p. A14)

distillation (dis′tə lā′shən) The process of separating the parts of a mixture by evaporation and condensation. (p. E64)

diversity (di vûr′si tē) A wide variety of traits in individuals from the same population. (p. A114)

Doppler effect (dop′lər i fekt′) The change in frequency (and pitch) as a source of sound moves toward or away from you. (p. F71)

downdraft (doun′draft′) A downward rush of air caused by the falling of rain during a thunderstorm. (pp. D55, D76)

echo (e′kō) A reflected sound wave. (p. F68)

echolocation (ek′ō lō kā′shən) Finding an object by using reflected sound. (p. F70)

ecological succession (ek′ə loj′i kəl sək sesh′ən) The gradual replacement of one community by another. (p. B82)

ecology (ē kol′ə jē) The study of how living and nonliving things interact. (p. B11)

ecosystem (ek′ō sis′təm) All the living and non-living things in an environment, including their interactions with each other. (p. B6)

effort arm (ef′ərt arm) The part of a lever that applies force to the resistance arm. (p. F26)

electromagnetic spectrum (i lek′trō mag net′ik spek′trəm) All the wavelengths of visible and invisible light in order, from short (gamma rays) to long (radio). (p. F119)

electromagnetism (i lek′trō mag′ni tiz′əm) The production of magnetism by electricity (and the production of electricity by magnets). (p. F118)

electron (i lek′tron) A particle in the space outside the nucleus of an atom that carries one unit of negative electric charge. (p. E27)

element (el′ə mənt) A pure substance that cannot be broken down into any simpler substances. (p. E22)

PRONUNCIATION KEY

a at; ā ape; ä far; âr care; ô law; e end; ē me; i it; ī ice; îr pierce; o hot; ō old; ôr fork; oi oil; ou out; u up; ū use; ü rule; ù pull; ûr turn; hw white; ng song; th thin; <u>th</u> this; zh measure; ə about, taken, pencil, lemon, circus

elevation (el′ə vā′shən) The height of a place above sea level. (p. C6)

embryo (em′brē ō′) The immature plant inside a seed. (p. A82)

emulsion (i mul′shən) A type of colloid in which one liquid is spread throughout another. (p. E60)

endangered species (en dān′jərd spē′shēz) A species that is in danger of becoming extinct. (p. B36)

epidermis (ep′i dûr′mis) An outermost layer of such plant parts as roots and leaves. (pp. A30, A34)

erosion (i rō′zhən) The picking up and carrying away of pieces of rocks. (p. C10)

evaporation (i vap′ə rā′shən) The slow changing of a liquid into a gas. (pp. B50, D38, E38)

evergreen (ev′ər grēn′) Said of a gymnosperm that keeps its leaves for at least a few years. *See* **deciduous**. (p. A69)

expand (ek spand′) To spread out, as when a material gets hotter. (p. E41)

extinct (ek stingkt′) A species that has died out completely. (p. B36)

F

fault (fôlt) A crack in Earth's crust whose sides show evidence of motion. (p. C6)

fault-block mountain (fôlt blok moun′tən) A mountain formed by blocks of Earth's crust moving along a fault. (p. C9)

fertilization (fûr′tə lə zā′shən) The joining of a sperm cell with an egg cell to make one new cell, a fertilized egg. (pp. A62, A81)

fertilizer (fûr′tə lī′zər) A substance used to add minerals to the soil. (p. B56)

fibrous root (fī′brəs rüt) One of the many hairy branching roots that some plants have. (p. A31)

filament (fil′ə mənt) The wire in a light bulb that gives off light and heat. (p. E92)

fish (fish) A vertebrate that lives its whole life in water. (p. A95)

flood plain (flud′ plān′) Land that is likely to be underwater during a flood. (p. C21)

foam (fōm) A type of colloid in which a gas is spread throughout a liquid. (p. E60)

fog (fôg) A cloud at ground level. (p. D44)

fold mountain (fōld moun′tən) A mountain made up mostly of rock layers folded by being squeezed together. (p. C8)

food chain (füd chān) The path of the energy in food from one organism to another. (p. B18)

food web (füd web) The overlapping food chains in an ecosystem. (p. B20)

force (fôrs) A push or pull exerted by one object on another, causing a change in motion. (p. F6)

fossil (fos′əl) Any remains or imprint of living things of the past. (p. C45)

fossil fuel (fos′əl fū′əl) A fuel formed from the decay of ancient forms of life. (p. C64)

fracture (frak′chər) The characteristic way some minerals break in uneven patterns. (p. C35)

freezing point (frēz′ing point) The temperature at which a substance changes state from a liquid to a solid. (p. E37)

frequency (frē′kwən sē) The number of times an object vibrates per second. (p. F57)

friction (frik′ shen′) A force that opposes the motion of one object moving past another. (p. F8)

frond (frond) The leaf of a fern. (p. A61)

front (frunt) A boundary between air masses with different temperatures. (p. D71)

fruit (früt) The ripened ovary of a flowering seed plant. (p. A70)

fulcrum (fül′krəm) The pivot point of a lever. (p. F26)

fundamental frequency (fun′də men′təl frē′kwən sē) The lowest frequency at which an object vibrates. (p. F72)

fungus (fung′gəs) *n.,* **fungi** (fun′jī) *pl.* Members of a kingdom that contains one-celled and many-celled living things that absorb food from their environment. (p. A17)

galaxy (gal′ək sē) A collection of billions of stars. Our Sun belongs to the Milky Way galaxy. (p. D20)

gas (gas) A form of matter that does not take up a definite amount of space and has no definite shape. (p. E36)

gel (jel) A type of colloid in which a solid is spread throughout a liquid. (p. E60)

gem (jem) A mineral valued for being rare and beautiful. (p. C38)

geologist (jē ol′ə jist) A scientist who studies rocks to tell how they formed and to predict when an earthquake may occur. (p. C16)

geothermal energy (jē′ō thûr′məl en′ər jē) Earth's internal energy. (p. C104)

germination (jûr′mə nā′shən) The sprouting of a seed into a new plant. (p. A83)

ginkgo (ging′kō) *n., pl.* **ginkgoes** A large gymnosperm with fan-shaped leaves. (p. A69)

gnetophyte (ne′tō fīt′) One of the gymnosperms that are closely related to flowering plants and live in both deserts and the tropics. (p. A69)

grassland (gras′land′) A biome where grasses, not trees, are the main plant life. Prairies are one kind of grassland region. (p. B66)

gravitropism (grav′ī trō′pi′zəm) The response of a plant to gravity. (p. A44)

gravity (grav′i tē) The force of attraction between any two objects due to their mass. (pp. D8, F35)

groundwater (ground wô′tər) Precipitation that seeps into the ground and is stored in tiny holes, or pores, in soil and rocks. (pp. B51, C74)

gymnosperm (jim′nə spûrm′) A seed plant that does not produce flowers. *See* **angiosperm.** (p. A68)

habitat (hab′i tat) The place where a plant or animal naturally lives and grows. (p. B12)

hail (hāl) Pellets made of ice and snow. (p. D47)

hardness (härd′nis) How well a mineral resists scratching. (p. C34)

herbivore (hûr′bə vôr′) An animal that eats plants, algae, and other producers. (p. B20)

heredity (hə red′i tē) The passing down of inherited traits from parents to offspring. (p. A110)

hertz (Hz) (hûrts) A unit for measuring frequency. One hertz equals a frequency of one vibration per second. (p. F57)

heterogeneous (het′ər ə jē′nē əs) Differing in kind or nature; dissimilar; not homogeneous. (p. E54)

high-pressure system (hī′presh′ər sis′təm) A pattern surrounding a high pressure center, from which winds blow outward. In the Northern Hemisphere these winds curve to the right in a clockwise pattern. (p. D59)

PRONUNCIATION KEY

a at; ā ape; ä far; âr care; ô law; e end; ē me; i it; ī ice; îr pierce; o hot; ō old; ôr fork; oi oil; ou out; u up; ū use; ü rule; u̇ pull; ûr turn; hw white; ng song; th thin; <u>th</u> this; zh measure; ə about, taken, pencil, lemon, circus

host (hōst) The organism a parasite lives in or on and is harmed by. (p. B26)

humidity (hū mid′i tē) The amount of water vapor in the air. (p. D38)

humus (hü′məs) Decayed plant or animal material in soil. (pp. B9, C49)

hurricane (hûr′i kān′) A very large, swirling storm with very low pressure at the center. (p. D78)

hybrid (hī′brid) An organism produced by the crossing of parents that have different forms of the same trait. (p. A112)

hydrocarbon (hī′drə kär′bən) Compound made only of hydrogen and carbon atoms. (p. E32)

hydroelectric plant (hī′drō i lek′trik plant) A factory where running or falling water spins a generator to make electricity. (p. C104)

hydrosphere (hī′drə sfîr′) Earth's water, found in continents and oceans, including the fresh water in ice, lakes, rivers, and underground water. (p. C26)

hydrotropism (hī drot′rə piz′əm) The response of a plant to a nearby source of water. (p. A45)

hyperthermia (hī′pər thûr′mē ə) The overheating of the body that can be caused by overexposure in a hot, dry climate. (p. D90)

I

igneous rock (ig′nē əs rok) A rock formed when melted rock material cools and hardens (p. C43)

image (im′ij) A "picture" of the light source that light rays make in bouncing off a polished, shiny surface. (p. F89)

imperfect flower (im pûr′fikt flou′ər) A flower with either a stamen or a pistil, but not both. (p. A78)

incomplete flower (in′kəm plēt′ flou′ər) A flower that lacks sepals, petals, stamens or pistils. (p. A78)

indicator (in′di kā′tər) A substance such as litmus paper whose color changes when it is mixed with an acid or a base. (p. E84)

inertia (i nûr′shə) The tendency of a moving object to keep moving in a straight line or of any object to resist a change in motion. (pp. D8, F7)

inexhaustible resource (in′eg zôs′tə bəl rē′sôrs′) A resource that cannot be depleted or used up easily. (p. B58)

inherited trait (in her′i təd trāt) A characteristic that is passed from parents to offspring. (p. A110)

inner planet (in′ər plan′it) A planet between the Sun and the asteroid belt (Mercury, Venus, Earth, Mars). (p. D16)

insolation (in′sə lā′shən) The amount of the Sun's energy that reaches Earth at a given time and place. *Insolation* is short for *in*coming *sol*ar radi*ation*. (p. D30)

instinct (in′stingkt′) An inherited behavior, one that is not learned but is done automatically. (p. A110)

insulate (in′sə lāt′) To prevent heat from passing through. (p. E14)

intertidal zone (in′tər tī′dəl zōn) The shallowest section of the marine, or ocean, ecosystem, where the ocean floor is covered and uncovered as the tide goes in and out. (p. B73)

invertebrate (in vûr′tə brit) An animal that does not have a backbone. (p. A16)

ionized (ī′ə nīzd′) Electrically charged by radiation, as gas particles of auroras in the night sky. (p. D32)

isobar (ī′sə bär′) A line on a weather map connecting places with equal air pressure. (p. D59)

K

kinetic energy (ki net′ik en′ər jē) The energy of any moving object. (p. E95)

land breeze (land brēz) Wind that blows from land to sea. (p. D56)

laser (lā'zər) A device that produces a thin stream of light of just a few close wavelengths. (p. F122)

lava (lä'və) Magma that reaches Earth's surface. (pp. C9, C43)

law of reflection (lô uv ri flek'shən) The angle between an incoming light ray and a surface equals the angle between the reflected light ray and the surface. (p. F87)

lever (lev'ər) A simple machine made of a rigid bar and a fixed pivot point, called the fulcrum. (p. F26)

light ray (līt rā) A straight-line beam of light as it travels outward from its source. (p. F85)

lightning (līt'ning) One of the huge electric sparks that leap from clouds to the ground in thunderstorms. (p. D76)

limiting factor (lim'ə ting fak'tər) Anything that controls the growth or survival of a population. (p. B34)

liquid (lik'wid) A form of matter that takes up a definite amount of space and has no definite shape. (p. E36)

lithosphere (lith'ə sfîr') The hard outer layer of Earth, about 100 km thick. (p. C26)

long-day plant (lông'dā plant) A plant that blooms when there is much more daylight than darkness. (p. A46)

low-pressure system (lō'presh'ər sis'təm) A pattern surrounding a low-pressure center, in which winds blow in toward the center. In the Northern Hemisphere, these winds blow to the right in a counterclockwise pattern. (p. D59)

luster (lus'tər) The way light bounces off a mineral's surface. (p. C33)

magma (mag'mə) Hot, molten rock deep below Earth's surface. (p. C9)

magnetic (mag net'ik) The property of a material like iron in which the particles line up pole to pole, causing it to be attracted or repelled by a magnet. (p. E15)

mammal (mam'əl) A vertebrate that feeds its young milk. (p. A95)

mare (mär'ā) *n., pl.* **maria** (mär'ē ə) Dark-colored land on the Moon that is dry and flat and is surrounded by mountains and ridges. (p. D10)

mass (mas) A measure of the amount of matter in an object. (p. E6)

matter (ma'tər) Anything that has mass and takes up space. (pp. E6, F51)

meander (mē an'dər) Bends or s-shaped curves in a river. (p. C21)

melting point (melt'ing point) The particular temperature for each substance at which it changes state from a solid to a liquid. (p. E37)

membrane (mem'brān) A thin envelope surrounding the nucleus of a cell. (p. A18)

metal (met'əl) Any of a group of elements found in the ground that conducts heat and electricity. (p. C38)

PRONUNCIATION KEY

a at; ā ape; ä far; âr care; ô law; e end; ē me; i it; ī ice; îr pierce; o hot; ō old; ôr fork; oi oil; ou out; u up; ū use;
ü rule; u̇ pull; ûr turn; hw white; ng song; th thin; <u>th</u> this; zh measure; ə about, taken, pencil, lemon, circus

metamorphic rock (met′ə môr′fik rok) A rock formed under heat and pressure from another kind of rock. (p. C46)

meteor (mē′ tē or) A chunk of rock from space that burns up as it travels through Earth's atmosphere. A "shooting star." (p. D19)

meteorite (mē′tē ə rīt′) A chunk of rock from space that strikes the surface of Earth or the Moon. (pp. C14, D19)

mid-ocean ridge (mid ō′shun rij) Chain of mountains that wind along all the world's major oceans. (p. C91)

mimicry (mim′i krē) An adaptation in which an animal is protected against predators by its resemblance to another, unpleasant animal. (p. A106)

mineral (min′ə rəl) A solid material of Earth's crust with a definite composition. (p. C32)

mixture (miks′chər) A physical combination of two or more substances that are blended together without forming new substances. (p. E52)

molecule (mol′ə kūl′) A particle that contains more than one atom joined together. (p. E30) *See* **atom.** (p. E26)

monocot (mon′ə kot′) An angiosperm with one cotyledon in each seed. *See* **dicot.** (p. A72)

mountain breeze (moun′tən brēz) A cool night wind that blows down a mountain slope to replace the warmer air in the valley. (p. D56)

mutualism (mū′chü ə liz′əm) A relationship between two kinds of organisms that benefits both. (p. B24)

N

neap tide (nēp tīd) The slightest changes from high to low tide that occur when the Sun, the Moon, and Earth form a right angle or are perpendicular to each other. (p. C89)

nekton (nek′tən) Organisms that swim through the water in aquatic ecosystems. (p. B72)

neutral (nü′trəl) Neither acid nor base. (p. E82)

neutron (nü′tron) A particle in the nucleus of an atom that has no net electric charge. (p. E27)

newton (nü′tən) A basic unit measuring the amount of pull or push a force produces. (pp. E7, F20)

NEXRAD (neks′rad′) A new form of Doppler radar that is used to track storms. The word stands for *NEXt generation of weather RADar.* (p. D81)

niche (nich) The role of an organism in a community. (p. B12)

nitrogen cycle (nī′trə jən sī′kəl) The continuous trapping of nitrogen gas into compounds in the soil and its return to the air. (p. B54)

nonrenewable resource (non′ri nü′ə bəl rē′sôrs′) A resource that cannot be replaced within a short period of time or at all. (pp. B58, C64)

nonvascular (non vas′kyə lər) Containing no plant tissue through which water and food move. (p. A15)

nucleus (nü′klē əs) **1.** A dense structure inside the cell. (p. A18) **2.** One of the airborne dust particles around which water condenses as droplets or ice crystals before falling as precipitation. (p. D46) **3.** An atom's dense center, where most of its mass is. (p. E27)

O

omnivore (om′nə vôr′) An animal that eats both plants and animals. (p. B21)

opaque (ō pāk′) Completely blocking light from passing through it. (p. F96)

orbit (ôr′bit) The path of a planet traveling around a star. (p. D6)

ore (ôr) A mineral containing a useful substance. (p. C38)

organ (ôr′gən) A group of tissues that work together to do a certain job. (p. A9)

organism (ôr′gə niz′əm) Any living thing that can carry out its life on its own. (p. A6)

organ system (ôr′gən sis′təm) A group of organs that work together to do a certain job. (p. A9)

outer planet (out′er plan′it) One of the five planets beyond the asteroid belt (Jupiter, Saturn, Uranus, Neptune, Pluto). (p. D16)

ovary (ō′və rē) A structure containing egg cells; thē base of a pistil in a flower. (p. A78)

overtone (ō′vər tōn′) One of a series of pitches that blend to give a sound its quality. (p. F72)

ozone layer (ō′zōn lā′ər) A layer of ozone gas in the atmosphere that screens out much of the Sun's UV (ultraviolet) rays. (p. C63)

P

parasitism (par′ə sī tiz′əm) A relationship in which one organism lives in or on another organism and benefits from that relationship while the other organism may be harmed by it. (p. B26) —**parasite** (par′ə sīt′) (pp. A71, B26)

perfect flower (pûr′fikt flou′ər) A flower with both male and female parts, that is, both a stamen and a pistil. (p. A78)

permafrost (pûr′mə frôst′) A layer of permanently frozen soil found in arctic and antarctic regions. (p. B68)

pH (pē′aitch′) The scale that tells how acidic or basic a solution is. (p. E86)

phloem (flō′em) The tissue through which food from the leaves moves down through the rest of a plant. (pp. A31, A32)

photon (fō′ton) The tiny bundles of energy by means of which light travels. (p. F119)

photoperiodism (fō′tō pîr′ē ə diz′əm) The flowering response of a plant to changing periods of daylight and darkness. (p. A46)

photosynthesis (fō′tə sin′thə sis) The food-making process in green plants that uses sunlight. (p. A36)

phototropism (fō tot′rə piz′əm) The response of a plant to changes in light. (p. A44)

phylum (fī′ləm) *n., pl.* **phyla** (-lə) One of the large groups in the animal kingdom. (p. A16)

physical change (fiz′i kəl chānj) A change of matter in size, shape, or state without any change in identity. (p. E70)

pioneer community (pī′ə nîr′ kə mū′ni tē) The first community thriving in a once lifeless area. (p. B83)

pioneer species (pī′ə nîr′ spē′shēz) The first species living in an otherwise lifeless area. (p. B83)

pitch (pich) How high or low a sound is. (p. F56)

planet (plan′it) Any of the nine major objects that travel around the Sun and shine by reflecting its light. (p. D6)

plankton (plangk′tən) Organisms that float on the water in aquatic ecosystems. (p. B72)

plate (plāt) One of the moving pieces of Earth's crust that has been broken by upward pressure from the mantle. (p. C7)

plate tectonics (plāt tek ton′iks) A scientific theory that Earth's crust is made of moving plates. (pp. B90, C7)

polarization (pō′lər ə zā′shən) Allowing light vibrations to pass through in only one direction. (p. F97)

pollen (pol′ən) Dustlike grains in the flower of a plant that contain its male sex cells. (pp. A70, A74, A84)

PRONUNCIATION KEY

a **at**; ā **ape**; ä **far**; âr **care**; ô **law**; e **end**; ē **me**; i **it**; ī **ice**; îr **pierce**; o **hot**; ō **old**; ôr **fork**; oi **oil**; ou **out**; u **up**; ū **use**; ü **rule**; ù **pull**; ûr **turn**; hw **white**; ng **song**; th **thin**; <u>th</u> **this**; zh **measure**; ə **about, taken, pencil, lemon, circus**

pollination (pol′ə nā′shən) The transfer of a pollen grain to the egg-producing part of a plant. (p. A74)

pollute (pə lüt′) v. To add harmful substances to Earth's land, water, or air. (p. C50) —**pollutant** (pə lü′tənt) n. Something that pollutes. (p. C50) —**pollution** (pə lü′shən) n. A polluted condition. (p. C50)

population (pop′yə lā′shən) All the members of one species in an area. (p. B11)

potential energy (pə ten′shəl en′ər jē) Stored energy. (p. E95)

precipitation (pri sip′i tā′shən) Any form of water particles that falls from the atmosphere and reaches the ground. (pp. B51, D46)

predator (pred′ə tər) An animal that hunts other animals for food. (pp. A106, B21)

prey (prā) A living thing that is hunted for food. (p. B21)

primary color (prī′mer′ē kul′ər) Red, green, or blue. Mixing these colors can produce all the colors of the spectrum. (p. F110)

primary pigment (prī′mer′ē pig′mənt) Magenta, cyan, or yellow. Materials with any of these colors absorb one primary color of light and reflect the other two. (p. F112)

primary succession (prī′mer′ē sək sesh′ən) The beginning of a community where few, if any, living things exist, or where earlier communities were wiped out. (p. B82)

prism (priz′əm) A cut piece of clear glass (or plastic) with two opposite sides in the shape of a triangle or other geometric shape. (p. F108)

producer (prə dü′sər) Any of the plants and algae that produce oxygen and food that animals need. (pp. B7, B20)

product (prod′ukt) A new substance produced by a chemical change. (p. E71)

prop root (prop rüt) One of the roots that grow out of a plant's stemlike main roots and help prop up the plant. (p. A31)

property (prop′ər tē) A characteristic of matter that can be observed, such as mass, volume, weight, or density. (pp. E6, E24)

protective coloration (prə tek′tiv kul′ə rā′shən) A type of camouflage in which the color of an animal blends in with its background, protecting it against predators. (p. A109)

protein (prō′tēn) A substance rich in nitrogen that the body uses for growth and the repair of cells. (p. B54)

protist (prō′tist) A member of a kingdom that contains one-celled and many-celled living things, some that make food and some that hunt for food. (p. A18)

proton (prō′ton) A particle in the nucleus of an atom that carries one unit of positive electric charge. (p. E27)

Q

quality (kwol′i tē) The difference you hear between two sounds of the same loudness and pitch. (p. F72)

R

radar (rā′där) A device for tracking the position and path of a distant moving object. (p. D80)

radiation (rā′dē a′shən) The transfer of heat through electromagnetic rays. (p. E97)

rarefaction (râr′ə fak′shən) The part of a sound wave where molecules are spread apart. (p. F51)

raw material (râ mə tîr′ē əl) Material not yet refined, manufactured, or processed. (p. B58)

reactant (rē ak′tənt) An original substance at the beginning of a chemical reaction. (p. E71)

reaction (rē ak′shən) The force with which an object responds to an action, as in Newton's third law of motion. (p. F24)

reflection (ri flek′shən) The bouncing of a sound wave off a surface. (p. F66)

refraction (ri frak′shən) The bending of light rays as they pass from one substance into another. (p. F98)

relative humidity (rel′ə tiv hū mid′i tē) A comparison between how much water vapor is in the air and how much the air could hold at a given temperature if it were full, or saturated. (p. D39)

renewable resource (ri nü′ə bəl rē′sôrs′) A resource that can be replaced in a short period of time. (pp. B58, C62)

reservoir (rez′ər vwär′) A storage area for fresh water supplies. (p. C75)

resistance arm (ri zis′təns arm) The part of a lever that applies force to the load the machine acts against. (p. F26)

resonance (rez′ə nəns) In an instrument or object, a unique blend of the fundamental frequency and its overtones. (p. F72)

resource (rē′sôrs′) Any material that helps support life on Earth. (p. C26)

respiration (res′pə rā′shən) The release of energy in plants and animals from food (sugar). (p. A37)

response (ri spons′) What a living thing does as a result of a stimulus. (p. A44)

reptile (rep′təl) An egg-laying vertebrate with thick, dry skin. (p. A95)

revolve (ri volv′) To move around, or orbit, another object. (p. D10)

rhizoid (rī′zoid) One of the hairlike fibers that anchor a moss to the soil and take in water from the soil. (p. A58)

rhizome (rī′zōm) The underground stem of a fern. (p. A61)

rock (rok) A naturally formed solid in the crust made up of one or more minerals. (p. C42)

rock cycle (rok sī′kəl) Rocks changing from one into another in a never-ending series of processes. (p. C52)

root cap (rüt kap) A thin covering made up of cells that protect the root tip of a plant as it grows into the soil. (p. A30)

root hair (rüt hâr) Any of the threadlike projections from a plant root that absorb water and dissolved minerals from the soil. (p. A30)

rotate (rō′tāt) To make a complete spin on an axis, causing one day on a planet. A day differs in length from planet to planet. (p. D9)

runoff (run′ôf) Precipitation that flows across the land's surface or falls into rivers and streams. (pp. B51, C20)

savanna (sə van′ə) A tropical grassland with some trees and shrubs. (p. B66)

scanning tunneling microscope (scan′ing tun′əl ing mī′krə skōp′) A device that uses electric current flowing through a needle to trace the contours of atoms and magnify them as much as 30 million times. (p. E26)

scavenger (skav′ən jər) A meat-eating animal that feeds on the remains of dead animals. (p. B21)

sea breeze (sē brēz) Wind that blows from sea to land. (p. D56)

sea-floor vent (sē′flôr′ vent) An opening in a mid-ocean ridge where mineral-saturated water boils up from the seafloor crust. (p. C93)

seamount (sē′mount′) A huge underwater volcanic mountain that may emerge from the ocean surface as an island. (p. C90)

PRONUNCIATION KEY

a **at**; ā **ape**; ä **far**; âr **care**; ô **law**; e **end**; ē **me**; i **it**; ī **ice**; îr **pierce**; o **hot**; ō **old**; ôr **fork**; oi **oil**; ou **out**; u **up**; ū **use**; ü **rule**; ù **pull**; ûr **turn**; hw **white**; ng **song**; th **thin**; <u>th</u> **this**; zh **measure**; ə **about, taken, pencil, lemon, circus**

secondary succession (sek'ən der'ē sək sesh'ən) The beginning of a new community where an earlier community already exists. (p. B82)

sediment (sed'ə ment) Pieces of material carried and deposited by water or wind (p. C20)

sedimentary rock (sed'ə men'tə rē rok) A rock made of bits of matter joined together. (p. C44)

seed (sēd) An undeveloped plant with stored food sealed in a protective covering. (p. A68)

seed coat (sēd kōt) The outer covering of a seed. (p. A82)

seed dispersal (sēd di spûr'səl) The movement of a seed from the flower to a place where it can sprout. (p. A83)

self-pollination (self'pol'ə nā'shən) The transfer of pollen from an anther to a stigma in the same plant. (p. A80)

sexual reproduction (sek'shü əl rē'prō duk'shən) The production of a new organism from a female sex cell and a male sex cell. (pp. A62, A81)

shear (shîr) A movement of plates that twists, tears, or pushes one part of Earth's crust past another. (p. C8)

short-day plant (shôrt'dā plant) A plant that blooms when there is more darkness and less daylight. (p. A46)

simple machine (sim'pəl mə shēn') A machine with few moving parts, making it easier to do work. (p. F26)

smog (smog) A mixture of smoke and fog. (p. C64)

solar system (sō'lər sis'təm) The Sun and the objects that are traveling around it. (p. D6)

solid (sol'id) A form of matter that has a definite shape and takes up a definite amount of space. (p. E36)

solubility (sol'yə bil'i tē) The ability of a substance to be dissolved by another substance. (p. E58)

solute (sol'ūt) A substance that is dissolved by another substance to form a solution. (p. E57)

solution (sə lü'shən) A mixture of substances that are blended so completely that the mixture looks the same everywhere. (p. E54)

solvent (sol'vənt) A substance that dissolves one or more other substances to form a solution. (p. E57)

sound wave (sound wāv) A vibration that spreads away from a vibrating object. (p. F51)

spectrum (spek'trəm) A band of colors produced when light goes through a prism. (p. F108)

speed (spēd) How fast an object's position changes with time at any given moment. (p. F11)

spore (spôr) Cells in seedless plants that grow into new organisms. (p. A58)

spring (spring) A place where groundwater seeps out of the ground. (p. C75)

spring tide (spring tīd) The greatest changes from high to low tide that occur when the Sun, the Moon, and Earth are lined up. (p. C89)

state of matter (stāt uv mat'ər) One of the three forms that matter can take—solid, liquid, or gas. (p. E36)

stimulus (stim'yə ləs), *n., pl.* **stimuli (-lī)** Something in the environment that causes a living thing to react. (p. A44)

stomata (stō'mə tə) *pl. n., sing.* **stoma** Pores in the bottom of leaves that open and close to let in air or give off water vapor. (p. A34)

storm surge (stôrm sûrj) A great rise of the sea along a shore caused by low air pressure. (p. D79)

stratus cloud (strā'təs kloud) A cloud that forms in a blanketlike layer. (p. D44)

streak (strēk) The color of the powder left when a mineral is rubbed against a hard, rough surface. (p. C34)

strip farming (strip fär'ming) Trapping runoff by alternating tightly growing grasses with more widely spaced plants. (p. C51)

subscript (sub'skript') A number in a chemical formula that tells the number of atoms in the compound. (p. E25)

surveyor (sər vā'ər) A specialist who makes accurate measurements of Earth's crust. (p. C6)

suspension (sə spen'shən) A mixture in which suspended particles can easily be seen. (p. E59)

symbiosis (sim'bē ō'sis) A relationship between two kinds of organisms that lasts over time. (p. B24)

T

taiga (tī'gə) A cool forest biome of conifers in the upper Northern Hemisphere. (p. B67)

taproot (tap'rüt') A root that has few hairy branches and grows deep into the ground. (p. A31)

temperate (tem'pər it) Free from extremes of temperature. (p. B66)

tension (ten'shən) A movement of plates that stretches or pulls apart Earth's crust. (p. C8)

terracing (ter'is ing) Shaping hillsides into steps so that runoff and eroded soil get trapped on the steps. (p. C51)

texture (teks'chər) An identifying quality of a rock based on how coarse, fine, or glassy it is and on how angular or rounded it is. (p. C42)

threatened species (thret'ənd spē'shēz) A species that is in danger of becoming endangered. (p. D36)

thunder (thun'dər) The noise caused by lightning-heated air during a thunderstorm. (p. D76)

thunderhead (thun'dər hed') A cumulonimbus cloud in which a thunderstorm forms. (p. D76)

thunderstorm (thun'dər stôrm') The most common severe storm, formed in cumulonimbus clouds. (p. D76)

tissue (tish'ü) A group of similar cells that work together at the same job. (p. A8)

topsoil (top'soil') The dark, top layer of soil, rich in humus and minerals, in which many tiny organisms live and most plants grow. (p. B9)

tornado (tôr nā'dō) A violent, whirling wind that moves across the ground in a narrow path. (p. D77)

trade wind (trād wind) A belt of winds around Earth moving from high pressure zones toward the low pressure at the equator. (p. D58)

translucent (trans lü'sənt) Letting only some light through, so that objects on the other side appear blurry. (p. F96)

transparent (trans pâr'ənt) Letting all light through, so that objects on the other side can be seen clearly. (p. F96)

transpiration (tran'spə rā'shən) The loss of water through a plant's leaves. (pp. A35, A38, D39)

trench (trench) A deep valley in the sea floor. (p. C91)

tropical rain forest (trop'i kəl rān fôr'ist) A hot biome near the equator, with much rainfall and a wide variety of life. (p. B71)

tropism (trō'piz'əm) A response of a plant toward or away from a stimulus. (p. A44)

PRONUNCIATION KEY

a at; ā ape; ä far; âr care; ô law; e end; ē me; i it; ī ice; îr pierce; o hot; ō old; ôr fork; oi oil; ou out; u up; ū use; ü rule; ù pull; ûr turn; hw white; ng song; th thin; <u>th</u> this; zh measure; ə about, taken, pencil, lemon, circus

troposphere (trop′ə sfîr′) The layer of the atmosphere closest to Earth's surface. (p. D32)

tube worm (tüb wûrm) Large wormlike animals that live near sea-floor vents and obtain their food through bacterial chemosynthesis. (p. C93)

tundra (tun′dra) Large, treeless plain in the arctic regions, where the ground is frozen all year. (p. B68)

ultrasonic (ul′trə son′ik) Said of a sound with a frequency too high to be heard by humans. (p. F57)

unbalanced forces (un bal′ənst fôrs′əz) Forces that do not cancel each other out when acting together on a single object. (p. F21)

updraft (up′draft′) An upward rush of heated air during a thunderstorm. (pp. D55, D76)

vacuum (vak′ū əm) A space through which sound waves cannot travel because it contains no matter. (p. F116)

valley breeze (val′ē brēz) A cool wind that blows up a mountain slope and replaces the slope's rising Sun-warmed air. (p. D56)

variable (vâr′ē ə bəl) One of the changes in a situation that may affect the outcome of an experiment. (p. A48)

vascular (vas′kyə lər) Containing plant tissue through which water moves up and food moves down. (p. A15)

velocity (və los′i tē) The speed and direction of a moving object. (p. F12)

vertebrate (vûr′tə brit) An animal that has a backbone. (p. A16)

vibration (vī brā′shən) A back-and-forth motion. (p. F50)

volume (vol′ūm) **1.** A measure of how much space an object takes up. (p. E6) **2.** The loudness or softness of a sound. (p. F58)

warm front (wôrm frunt) A front where warm air moves in over a cold air mass. (p. D72)

water cycle (wô′tər sī′kəl) The continuous movement of water between Earth's surface and the air, changing from liquid to gas to liquid. (pp. B51, C74)

water table (wô′tər tā′bəl) The top of the water-filled spaces in the ground. (p. C75)

water vapor (wô′tər vā′pər) Water in the form of a gas. (pp. B50, D38)

watershed (wô′tər shed′) Area from which water is drained; region that contributes water to a river or river system. (pp. C20, C68–C69)

weather (weth′ər) What the lower atmosphere is like at any given place and time. (p. D34)

weathering (weth′ər ing) Breaking down rocks into smaller pieces. (p. C10)

weight (wāt) The force of gravity between Earth and an object. (pp. E7, F36)

well (wel) A hole dug below the water table that water seeps into. (p. C75)

wind (wind) Air that moves horizontally. (p. D55)

work (wûrk) The use of force to move an object a certain distance. (p. F26)

xylem (zī′ləm) The tissue through which water and minerals move up through a plant. (pp. A30, A32)

year (yîr) The time it takes a planet to orbit the Sun. A *year* is different from planet to planet. (p. D7)

Index

* Indicates an activity related to this topic.

*Indicates an activity related to this topic.

*Indicates an activity related to this topic.

*Indicates an activity related to this topic.

*Indicates an activity related to this topic.

*Indicates an activity related to this topic.

*Indicates an activity related to this topic.

*Indicates an activity related to this topic.

Credits

Cover Photos: Chris Johns/National Geographic; bkgd. ThinkStock/Superstock.

Photography Credits: All photographs are by Macmillan/McGraw-Hill (MMH) except as noted below:

Unit A: A0 (bkgd) Kelvin Aitken/Peter Arnold Inc; A1 (bkgd) Norbert Wu/Norbert Wu; A1 (br) Kelvin Aitken/Peter Arnold Inc; A2-A3 (bkgd) Gallo Images/Corbis; A4 (bkgd) Ted Levin/Animals Animals/Earth Scenes; A5 (br) Richard Hutchings for MMH; A6 (bl) Peter Miller/Photo Researchers, Inc.; A7 (br) Dick Thomas/Visuals Unlimited; A9 (b) Rob Hadlow/Bruce Coleman, Inc.; A12 Carol Cohen/Corbis; A13 (br) Ken Karp for MMH; A17 (bc) Doug Sokell/Visuals Unlimited; A17 (bcl) Veronika Burmeister/Visuals Unlimited; A17 (bcr) R.M. Meadows/Peter Arnold, Inc.; A18 (bc) Veronika Burmeister/Visuals Unlimited; A18 (bcl) Patrick W. Grace/Science Source/Photo Researchers, Inc.; A18 (bcr) Cabisco/Visuals Unlimited; A18 (bl) Gilbert S. Grant/Photo Researchers, Inc.; A18 (br) R. Kessel-G. Shih/Visuals Unlimited; A19 (bcl) Telegraph Colour Library/FPG/Getty Images; A19 (bcr) A. & F. Michler/Peter Arnold, Inc.; A19 (bl) R. Robinson/Visuals Unlimited; A20 (b) Jim Roetzel/Dembinsky Photo Associates; A20 (bc) Skip Moody/Dembinsky Photo Associates; A20 (br) John Shaw/Bruce Coleman, Inc.; A20 (c) John Cancalosi/Peter Arnold, Inc.; A20 (cr) E.R. Degginger/Color-Pic, Inc.; A21 (cr) Manfred Kage/Peter Arnold, Inc.; A25 (cl) Hans Reinhard/Bruce Coleman, Inc.; A26 (bkgd) William Waterfall/The Stock Market/CORBIS; A28-9 (bkgd) Dominique Braud/Dembinsky Photo Associates; A29 (br) Richard Hutchings/Dembinsky Photo Associates; A33 (b) Willard Clay/Dembinsky Photo Associates; A33 (tl) George Bernard/Animals Animals/Earth Scenes; A33 (tr) ©Robert Maier/Animals Animals/Earth Scenes; A36 (t) PHOTODISC/Getty Images; A38 (bl) Jack M. Bostrack/Visuals Unlimited; A38 (br) Jack M. Bostrack/Visuals Unlimited; A38 (cr) Gerry Ellis/ENP Images; A39 (tl) Phil Degginger/Color-Pic, Inc.; A41 (cr) James R. Holland/National Geographic Society; A42-A43 Kalpana Kartik/Alamy Images; A44 (b) David Newman/Visuals Unlimited; A45 (tr) R. Calentine/Visuals Unlimited; A47 (b) Bill Beatty/Visuals Unlimited; A47 (tr) Parke H. John, Jr./Visuals Unlimited; A49 Royalty-Free/CORBIS; A50-1 (bkgd) Jim Olive/Pictor/Uniphoto; A51 (cr) WHM Bildarchiv/Peter Arnold, Inc.; A51 (tcr) Hans Reinhard/Bruce Coleman, Inc.; A51 (tl) Prof. K. Banks/©courtesy of Katherine Banks; A53 (cl) David Newman/Visuals Unlimited; A54 (bkgd) Bob Krist/CORBIS; A56-7 (bkgd) ©Michael Fogden/Bruce Coleman, Inc.; A57 (br) Richard Hutchings for MMH; A58 (bcl) John Trager/Visuals Unlimited; A58 (bcr) David Sieren/Visuals Unlimited; A58 (cl) Doug Sokell/Visuals Unlimited; A59 (bcl) Ed Reschke/Peter Arnold, Inc.; A59 (c) Mike Perry/Pictor/Uniphoto; A60 (b) Richard Hutchings for MMH; A60 (t) Richard Hutchings for MMH; A61 David Dennis/Animals Animals/Earth Scenes; A64 (tcr) Dick Keen/Visuals Unlimited; A65 (tc) E.R. Degginger/Color-Pic, Inc.; A66-7 (bkgd) Michael Gadomski/Animals Animals/Earth Scenes; A67 (br) Richard Hutchings for MMH; A68 (bl) Jim Hughes/Visuals Unlimited; A68 (br) V.P. Weinland/Photo Researchers, Inc.; A68 (c) W. Ormerod/Visuals Unlimited; A69 (bc) Gerald & Buff Corsi/Visuals Unlimited; A69 (br) E. Webber/Visuals Unlimited; A69 (inset) John N. Trager/Visuals Unlimited; A69 (l) Jan Taylor/Bruce Coleman, Inc.; A69 (r) E.R. Degginger/Bruce Coleman, Inc.; A70 (tl) Scott T. Smith/CORBIS; A71 (b) V. McMillan/Visuals Unlimited; A71 (t) E.F. Anderson/Visuals Unlimited; A73 (b) Visuals Unlimited/©Arthur R. Hill/VU; A73 (r) Mark S. Skalny/Visuals Unlimited; A74 (tl) SIME s.a.s./E-stock Photo; A75 (r) PhotoDisc; A76-7 (bkgd) Robert P. Carr/Bruce Coleman, Inc.; A77 (br) Richard Hutchings for MMH; A79 (b) Adam Jones/Photo Researchers, Inc.; A79 (cl) Doug Sokell/Visuals Unlimited; A79 (tl) Derrick Ditchburn/Visuals Unlimited; A82 (b) Henry T. Kaiser/Pictor/Uniphoto; A83 (cr) Stephen J. Lang/Visuals Unlimited; A83 (tc) Inga Spence/Visuals Unlimited; A83 (tr) Ken Wagner/Visuals Unlimited; A84 (tc) Jerome Wexler/Photo Researchers, Inc.; A84 (tl) John Gerlach/Visuals Unlimited; A89 (bl) Hans Reinhard/Bruce Coleman, Inc.; cl) John McAnulty/CORBIS; A90-1 (bkgd) R&V Taylor/Bruce Coleman, Inc.; A92-A93 ABPL/HAAGNER, CLEM/Animals Animals; A94 (b) ZEFA/Rauschenbach/Masterfile; A94 (t) Fred Bavendam/Minden Pictures; A95 (bl) BIOS Klein/Hubert/Peter Arnold, Inc.; A95 (tr) Joe McDonald/Bruce Coleman, Inc.; A96 (bcl) Tom E. Adams/Peter Arnold, Inc.; A96 (br) E.R. Degginger/Color-Pic, Inc.; A96 (cl) Scott Johnson/Animals Animals/Earth Scenes; A96 (tc) Jeff Mondragon/Mondragon Photography; A96 (tcr) E.R. Degginger/Color-Pic, Inc.; A96 (tl) Susan Blanchet/Dembinsky Photo Associates; A97 (bcl) Breck P. Kent/Animals Animals/Earth Scenes; A97 (bcr) Pictor/Uniphoto; A97 (br) Fred Bavendam/Peter Arnold, Inc.; A97 (c) Robert Lubeck/Animals Animals/Earth Scenes; A97 (cl) Jeff J. Daly/Stock Boston; A97 (cr) Fred Bavendam/Peter Arnold, Inc.; A97 (t) Hans Pfletschinger/Peter Arnold, Inc.; A98 (bcl) Norbert Wu/Peter Arnold, Inc.; A98 (bl) Skip Moody/Dembinsky Photo Associates; A98 (br) Gary Meszaros/Bruce Coleman, Inc.; A98 (cr) Marilyn Kazmers/Dembinsky Photo Associates; A98 (tcr) UNIPHOTO, Inc./Pictor/Uniphoto; A98 (tl) Zig Leszczynski/Animals Animals/Earth Scenes; A99 (bcr) Bob Cranston/Animals Animals/Earth Scenes; A99 (br) Rob Simpson/Pictor/Uniphoto; A99 (c) Des & Jen Bartlett/Bruce Coleman, Inc.; A99 (cl) E.R. Degginger/Color-Pic, Inc.; A99 (tc) Michael Newman/PhotoEdit; A99 (tcl) Darrell Gulin/CORBIS; A99 (tr) UNIPHOTO, Inc./Pictor/Uniphoto; A100 (b) Ken Karp for MMH; A101 (c) Graham Pizzey/Bruce Coleman, Inc.; A104 (bkgd) John Gerlach/Dembinsky Photo Associates; A104 (inset) Rolf Kopfle/Bruce Coleman, Inc.; A105 (A106 (bl) L. West/Bruce Coleman, Inc.; A106 (br) Stan W. Elems/Visuals Unlimited; A106 (tr) Visuals Unlimited/©Stan W. Elems/VU; A107 (bl) E.R. Degginger/Color-Pic, Inc.; A107 (cl) Visuals Unlimited/©Stan W. Elems/VU; A107 (cr) Rod Planck/Dembinsky Photo Associates; A108 (b) Steve Kaufman/Peter Arnold, Inc.; A109 (t) Kim Taylor/Bruce Coleman, Inc.; A110 (tl) E.R. Degginger/Color-Pic, Inc.; A110 (tr) E.R. Degginger/Color-Pic, Inc.; A110-1 (b) D. Robert Franz/Bruce Coleman, Inc.; A111 (br) Erwin & Peggy Bauer/Bruce Coleman, Inc.; A111 (tc) John Shaw/Bruce Coleman, Inc.; A111 (tl) John Snyder/Bruce Coleman, Inc.; A111 (tr) Skip Moody/Dembinsky Photo Associates; A112 (cl) E.R. Degginger/Color-Pic, Inc.; A112 (tc) E.R. Degginger/Color-Pic, Inc.; A112 (tl) Randa Bishop/Pictor/Uniphoto; A113 (bc) Image Bank/Getty Images; A113 (bl) Akira Matoba; A113 (br) Shoot Photography/Image State; A114 (b) Stan Osolinski/Dembinsky Photo Associates; A115 (tcr) Gerard Lacz/Animals Animals/Earth Scenes; A117 (tcl) Stan W. Elems/Visuals Unlimited; A19 (br) Blair Seitz/Photo Researchers, Inc.; A59 (cr) E.F.Anderson/Visuals Unlimited.

Unit B: B0-1 (bkgd) Art Wolfe/Stone; B1 (br) Tim Flach/Stone; B2-3 (bkgd) Lee Rentz/Bruce Coleman, Inc.; B4-5 (bkgd) Zig Leszczynski/Animals Animals/Earth Scenes; B5 (br) Richard Hutchings for MMH; B8 (b) John Shaw/Bruce Coleman, Inc.; B8-9 (t) John Shaw/Bruce Coleman, Inc.; BO (bkgd) Tim Flach/Stone; B10 (cl) John Giustina/Bruce Coleman, Inc.; B10 (cr) Joe McDonald/CORBIS; B10 (t) David J. Sams/Stock Boston; B11 (b) Lee Rentz/Bruce Coleman, Inc.; B12 (b) Robert M. Balou/Animals Animals/Earth Scenes; B12 (b) Laura Riley/Bruce Coleman, Inc.; B13 (b) PhotoDisc/Getty Images; B14 (b) James Carmichael/Bruce Coleman, Inc.; B22 (b) Joe McDonald/Bruce Coleman, Inc.; B22 (cl) Larry West/ Bruce Coleman Inc; B22 (cr) Gary Braasch/Stone/Getty Images; B23 (bl) Scott Smith/Animals Animals; B23 (tr) Doug Wechsler/Animals Animals; B24 (t) M.P.L. Fogden/Bruce Coleman, Inc.; B24-5 (b) Mark Newman/Bruce Coleman, Inc.; B26 (bcl) E.R. Degginger/ Animals Animals; B26 (bl) Image Club; B26 (br) John Shaw/Bruce Coleman, Inc.; B26 (tr) David Overcash/Bruce Coleman, Inc.; B27 (bl) Patty Murray/Earth Scenes; B27 (t) Lawrence Naylor/Photo Researchers; B30 (c) John Pontier/Animals Animals; B30 (t) Jeff Foote/Bruce Coleman, Inc.; B32-3 (bkgd) James Randklev/Stone/Getty Images; B33 (br) Richard Hutchings for MMH; B34 (bl) John Shaw/Bruce Coleman, Inc.; B34 (br) B&C Calhoun/Bruce Coleman, Inc.; B35 (b) Jeff Foott/Bruce Coleman, Inc.; B36 (tr) N.E. Swedberg/Bruce Coleman, Inc.; B37 (br) Joe McDonald/Animals Animals/Earth Scenes; B38 (tr) Buddy Mays/Corbis; B39 (bl) Steve Dunwell/Index Stock; B39 (tr) Creation Captured/Index Stock; B40 (t) John H. Hoffman/Bruce Coleman, Inc.; B42 (t) Lynn Funkhouser/Peter Arnold, Inc.; B42-3 (bkgd) Joe Sroka/Dembinsky Photo Associates; B43 (cl) Kelvin Aitken/Peter Arnold, Inc.; B43 (cr) Fred Bavendam/Peter Arnold, Inc.; B46-7 (bkgd) Kennan Ward/The Stock Market/CORBIS; B48-9 (bkgd) John Shaw/Bruce Coleman, Inc.; B49 (br) Richard Hutchings for MMH; B56 (t) E.R. Degginger/Earth Scenes; B57 (bc) Cesar Llacuna for MMH; B57 (bl) Cesar Llacuna for MMH; B59 (tcr) Peter Beck/The Stock Market/CORBIS; B62-3 (bkgd) UNIPHOTO, Inc./Pictor; B63 (br) Richard Hutchings for MMH; B64 (c) Nigel J.H. Smith/Earth Scenes; B64 (t) Breck P. Kent/Earth Scenes; B64 (tc) Lee Rentz/Rentl/Bruce Coleman, Inc.; B65 (br) M. Timothy O'Keefe/Bruce Coleman, Inc.; B65 (tl) J.C. Carton/Bruce Coleman, Inc.; B65 (tr) Eastcott/Momatiuk/Earth Scenes; B66 (t) A.&M. Shah/Animals Animals; B67 (b) Eastcott/Momatiuk/Earth Scenes; B68 (t) Joe McDonald/Bruce Coleman, Inc.; B68-9 (c) Joy Spurr/Bruce Coleman, Inc.; B69 (bl) Jen & Des Bartlett/Bruce Coleman, Inc.; B70 (bl) Jeff Foott/Bruce Coleman, Inc.; B70 (b) John Shaw/Bruce Coleman, Inc.; B71 (br) E&P Bauer/Bruce Coleman, Inc.; B71 (tr) Joe McDonald/CORBIS; B72 (bl) PhotoDisc/Getty Images; B74 (t) M. Newman/Bruce Coleman, Inc.; B78-9 (bkgd) Gary Braasch/CORBIS; B79 (br) Danny Lehman/CORBIS; B80 (tr) John Elk III/Bruce Coleman, Inc.; B82 (t) The Image Bank/Getty Images. B82 (br) David Falconer/Bruce Coleman, Inc. B83 (bl) John Lemker/Earth Scenes; B83 Gibson Stock Photography; B85 (l) E.R. Degginger/Earth Scenes; B85 (r) PhotoDisc/Getty Images; B86 (b) E.R. Degginger/Earth Scenes; B86 (t) S. Jonasson/Bruce Coleman, Inc.; B87 (br) Richard Hutchings for MMH; B88 (t) Tom Bean/CORBIS; B88-9 (b) Bob Burch/Bruce Coleman, Inc.; B91 (b) John Elk III/Bruce Coleman, Inc.;

B16-7 (bkgd) Beverly Joubert/National Geographic Collection/GettyOne Images.

Unit C: C0 (bkgd) Jules Cowan/Index Stock Imagery; C1 (bkgd) Jules Cowan/Index Stock Imagery; C2-3 (bkgd) Peter French/Bruce Coleman, Inc.; C4-5 (bkgd) AFB/CORBIS; C5 (br) Richard Hutchings for MMH; C6 (b) John D. Cunningham/Visuals Unlimited; C6 (inset) Sinclair Stammers/Science Photo Library/Photo Researchers, Inc.; C9 (bl) Dr. E.R. Degginger/Color-Pic, Inc.; C9 (tr) Stella Snead/Bruce Coleman, Inc.; C10 (bl) Jerry Schad/Photo Researchers, Inc.; C10 (br) Jim Steinberg/Photo Researchers, Inc.; C10 (tr) Jeff Greenberg/Index Stock Imagery; C11 (bl) Gilbert Grant/Photo Researchers, Inc.; C11 (tr) ©Zandria Muench Beraldo/CORBIS; C12 (b) Renee Lynn/Photo Researchers, Inc.; C13 (t) Terranova International/Photo Researchers, Inc.; C14 (b) Detlev van Ravenswaay/Photo Researchers; C14 (c) John Chumack/PRI; C14 (t) NASA/PhotoTake; C18-9 (bkgd) ©Walter Bibikow/Index Stock Imagery; C20 (b) ©Jim Wark/Index Stock Imagery; C20 (tr) ©Mick Roessler/Index Stock Imagery; C21 (t) Yann Arthus-Bertrand/Corbis; C22 (b) Bob Krist/Corbis; C22 (cr) ©Jules Cowan/Index Stock Imagery; C23 (tl) ©Diaphor Agency/Index Stock Imagery; C24 (tr) NASA/Goddard Space Flght Center, The SeaWiFs Project and ORBIMAGE, Scientific Visualization Studio; C26 (cr) NASA/NASA; C27 (tr) Randy Faris/Corbis; C28 (b) Mark Mellett//Stock, Boston; C28-9 (t) Dave Bartruff/Stock, Boston; C29 (tl) Annie Griffiths Belt/Bettmann/Corbis; C29 (tr) Morton Beebe,S.F./Bettmann/Corbis; C30-1 (bkgd) George Lepp/CORBIS; C32 (bc) Charles D. Winters/Timeframe Photography Inc./Photo Researchers, Inc.; C32 (bcl) Cesar Llacuna for MMH; C32 (bcr) Function Thru Form; C32 (c) Joyce Photographics/Photo Researchers, Inc.; C32 (cl) E. R. Degginger/Photo Researchers, Inc.; C32 (cr) George Whiteley/Photo Researchers, Inc.; C33 (bc) Cesar Llacuna for MMH; C33 (bcl) David Lees/CORBIS; C33 (bcr) Cesar Llacuna for MMH; C33 (c) Kaj R. Svensson/Science Photo Library/Photo Researchers, Inc.; C33 (cl) Roberto De Gugliemo/Science Photo Library/Photo Researchers, Inc.; C33 (cr) J.H. Robinson/Photo Researchers, Inc.; C34 (tc) Mark A. Schneider/Visuals Unlimited; C34 (tl) John D. Cunningham/Visuals Unlimited; C34 (tr) Tom Pantages/PhotoTake; C35 (tl) A.J. Cunningham/Visuals Unlimited; C36 (bl) Ross Frid/Korner Gems, Traverse City, MI/Visuals Unlimited; C36 (br) Charles O'Rear/CORBIS; C36 (c) Joyce Photographics/Photo Researchers, Inc.; C36 (tr) A.J.Copley/Visuals Unlimited; C37 (tl) Peter Aitken/Photo Researchers, Inc.; C38 (bcl) A.J. Copley/Visuals Unlimited; C38 (bl) David Young-Wolff/PhotoEdit/PictureQuest; C38 (cr) Color Image/SuperStock; C38 (tr) Richard T. Nowitz/Photo Researchers, Inc.; C40-1 (bkgd) Lee Rentz/Bruce Coleman, Inc.; C41 (br) Richard Hutchings for MMH; C42 (bc) Doug Sokell/Visuals Unlimited; C42 (bl) Andrew J. Martinez/Photo Researchers, Inc.; C42 (br) Andrew J. Martinez/Photo Researchers, Inc.; C43 (bl) E.R. Degginger/Photo Researchers, Inc.; C43 (br) AJ Copley/Visuals Unlimited; C44 (bcr) Joyce Photographics/Photo Researchers, Inc.; C44 (bl) Andrew J. Martinez/Photo Researchers, Inc.; C44 (br) ©A.J. Copley/VU; C44 (tcr) Martin G. Miller/Visuals Unlimited; C44 (tr) Andrew J. Martinez/Photo Researchers, Inc.; C45 (b) John D. Cunningham/Visuals Unlimited; C45 (bl) Joyce Photographics/Photo Researchers, Inc.; C45 (cl) Kjell B. Sandved/Photo Researchers, Inc.; C46 (bl) E.R. Degginger/Photo Researchers, Inc.; C46 (br) Charles R. Belinky /Photo Researchers, Inc.; C46 (tl) Arthur R. Hill/Visuals Unlimited; C46 (tr) L.S. Stepanowicz/Visuals Unlimited; C47 (c) Michael P. Gadomski/Photo Researchers, Inc.; C48 (br) Joyce Photographics/Photo Researchers, Inc.; C48 (inset) Joyce Photographics/Photo Researchers, Inc.; C50 (bl) G. Büttner/Naturbild/OKAPIA/Photo Researchers, Inc.; C51 (tl) Ron Spomer/Visuals Unlimited; C53 (cr) John Elk III/Stock, Boston; C57 (cr) Detlev van Ravenswaay/The Stock Market/CORBIS; C58-9 (bkgd) Paul Steel/The Stock Market; C60-1 (bkgd) NASA; C61 (br) Richard Hutchings for MMH; C62 (bl) Photodisc/Getty Images; C64 (br) Hattie Young/Science Photo Library/Photo Researchers, Inc.; C64 (tl) Phil Degginger/Color-Pic, Inc.; C64 (tr) Gary Withey/Bruce Coleman, Inc.; C65 (b) Simon Fraser/Science Photo Library/Photo Researchers, Inc.; C67 (br) Chase Swift/Corbis; C67 (tr) McGraw-Hill School Division/; C70-1 (bkgd) IFA/Peter Arnold, Inc.; C71 (br) Richard Hutchings for MMH; C73 (t) Calvin Larsen/Photo Researchers, Inc.; C76 (b) Simon Fraser/Science Photo Library/Photo Researchers, Inc.; C77 (br) Richard Hutchings for MMH; C82-3 (bkgd) Dave G. Houser/PICTOR/Image State; C84 (tc) L.Lipsky/Bruce Coleman, Inc.; C84-5 (t) VCG/FPG/Getty Images; C85 (tc) Jan Stromme/Bruce Coleman, Inc.; C86 (cr) NASA/Tom Pantages; C87 (t) Ira Rubin/Dembinsky Photo Associates; C88 (b) Jeff Greenberg/PhotoEdit; C92 (b) Emory Kristof/National Geographic/Getty Images; C92 (tr) R&V Taylor/Bruce Coleman, Inc.; C93 (tr) Norbert Wu/Norbert Wu Productions; C94 (br) Fulvio Eccardi/Bruce Coleman, Inc.; C94 (t) Chinch Gryniewicz/Ecoscene/CORBIS; C95 (cr) PhotoDisc; C98-9 (bkgd) Ron Sherman/Stock Boston, Inc.; C99 (br) Richard Hutchings for MMH; C100 (bl) Phil Degginger/Color-Pic, Inc.; C100 (br) Joseph Nettis/Photo Researchers, Inc.; C101 (t) Ted Speigel/Bettmann/CORBIS; C104 (bl) Simon Fraser/Science Photo Library/Photo Researchers, Inc.; C104 (tr) Phil Degginger/Color-Pic, Inc.;

C104-5 (b) Russell D. Curtis/Photo Researchers, Inc.; C105 (br) Kevin Schafer/Peter Arnold, Inc.; C105 (tl) John Keating/Photo Researchers, Inc.; C106 (tl) Patrick Grace/Photo Researchers, Inc.; C107 (cr) Matt Meadows/Peter Arnold, Inc.; C109 (tr) John Keating/Photo Researchers, Inc.

Unit D: D0 (bkgd) NOAA, colored by John Wells/Science Photo Library/Photo Researchers Inc; D1 (bkgd) World Perspectives/Stone; D2-3 Courtesy NASA/JPL-CalTech; D4 STSI/Photo Researchers Inc; D5 (br) Richard Hutchings for MMH; D7 (cl) Richard Hutchings for MMH; D10 (b) Science VU/Visuals Unlimited; D12 (tr) Pekka Parviainen/Dembinsky Photo Associates; D13 (cr) E.Karkoschka (Univ. of Az.) /NASA; D14 Courtesy NASA/ JPL-CalTech; D16 USGS/Photo Researchers, Inc.; D16 NASA/Science Source/Photo Researchers, Inc.; D16 USGS /Photo Researchers, Inc.; D18 (l) NASA/Photo Researchers, Inc.; D19 (l) NASA and Erich Karkoschka, University of Arizona; D19 (r) NASA/Phototake/Alamy Images; D20 (r) Ron Russell/Index Stock; D22 (bkgd) n/a; D22 (br) JPL/NASA; D23 (tl) NASA; D23 (tr) Photo Researchers, Inc.; D25 (bl) Ron Russell/Index Stock; D26 (b) Steve Terrill/The Stock Market/CORBIS; D28 (bkgd) G.L. Kooyman/Animals Animals/Earth Scenes; D28 (br) Price, R. -Surv. OSF/Animals Animals/Earth Scenes; D29 (br) Richard Hutchings for MMH; D34 (tcl) Runk/Schoenberger/Grant Heilman Photography, Inc.; D34 (tr) Yoav Levy/PhotoTake; D35 (tr) E.R. Degginger/Color-Pic, Inc.; D36 (bkgd) Wolfgang Kaehler/CORBIS; D37 (b) Richard Hutchings for MMH; D42 (bkgd) Bonnie Kamin/PhotoEdit; D43 (b) Richard Hutchings Photography/Richard Hutchings; D44 (br) Visuals Unlimited/©Mark A. Schneider/VU; D44 (cr) Visuals Unlimited/©Henry W. Robison/VU; D44 (tr) Visuals Unlimited/©A.J. Copley/VU; D46 (bcr) Visuals Unlimited/©Mark E. Gibson/VU; D46 (bl) Visuals Unlimited/©D. Cavagnaro/VU; D46 (bcl) Visuals Unlimited/©W. Banaszewski/VU; D46 (br) Corbis/Corbis/Bettmann; D47 (br) Dembinsky Photo Associates/©Michael P. Gadomski; D47 (cr) Fundamental Photographs/©Jeff J. Daly; D49 (tr) McGraw-Hill School Division/; D51 (tl) Corbis/©Sean Sexton/COBBIS; D52 (bkgd) Corbis/©Vince Streano/CORBIS; D53 (br) Hutchings/Richard Hutchings; D55 (b) Superstock/©Superstock; D56 (t) The Stock Market/©TSM/Torleif Svensson; D58 (bl) NASA. (br) Hutchings/Richard Hutchings; D61 (tcr) Corbis/©Paul A. Souders/CORBIS; D61 (tr) McGraw-Hill School Division/; D66 (bkgd) Animals Animals/Earth Scenes/©Stephen Ingram; D68 (bkgd) Animals Animals/Earth Scenes/©Bertram G. Murray JR; D73 (tr) Animals Animals/Earth Scenes/©Charles Palek; D77 (cr) Richard Hutchings Photography/Richard Hutchings; D79 (b) Visuals Unlimited/©Science VU; D80 (bl) Peter Arnold, Inc./©NOAA/Peter Arnold, Inc.; D80 (br) Carlos Guerrero/Carlos Guerrero; D82 (bkgd) Animals Animals/Earth Scenes/©Arthur Gloor; D85 (br) Hutchings/Richard Hutchings; D87 Benelux Press/Index Stock; D88 (l) Visuals Unlimited/©Science VU; D88 (r) Visuals Unlimited/©VU; D89 Superstock; D90 (br) PhotoEdit/Jeff Greenberg; D90 (tr) Tony Stone Images/©Don Smetzer/TSI; D91 (cr) Bridgeman Art Library Int'l Ltd/Frost Fair on the Thames, Abraham Hondius, Museum of London, UK, The Bridgeman Art Library D93 (bcl) Dembinsky Photo Associates/©Mark A. Schneider;

Unit E: E0 (bkgd) Roger Ressmeyer/CORBIS; E2-E3 (bkgd) ©Christine Osborne/CORBIS; E4-E5 (bkgd) ©Michael T. Sedam/CORBIS; E5 (br) Richard Hutchings; E6 (b) ©Ken Karp/McGraw-Hill School Division; E8 (bl) ©Ken Karp/McGraw-Hill School Division; E8 (br) ©Ken Karp/McGraw-Hill School Division; E8 (c) Ken Karp/McGraw-Hill School Division; E9 (br) Richard Hutchings; E11 (bcr) Wolfgang Kaehler/Bettman/CORBIS; E11 (bl) Buddy Mays/Bettman/CORBIS; E11 (tc) George Bernard/Photo Researchers, Inc.; E11 (tl) /Klaus Guldbrandsen/ Science Photo Library/Photo Researchers, Inc.; E11 Sinclair Stammers/Science Photo Library/Photo Researchers; E11 Chris McElcheran/Masterfile; E13 (tr) ©Carl Purcell/Photo Researchers, Inc.; E14 (bl) ©Kim Sayer/CORBIS; E14 (br) Phil Degginger/Color-Pic, Inc.; E14 (tr) Phil Degginger/Color-Pic, Inc.; E15 PhotoDisc; E16 (b) ©National Railway of Japan/ PhotoTake; E16 (cr) IBM Research/Peter Arnold, Inc.; E16 (tr) Lawrence Livermore National Laboratory/Science Photo Library/Photo Researchers, Inc.; E17 (bcr) McGraw-Hill School Division; E18 (bkgd) Rod Plack/Photo Researchers, Inc.; E20 (bkgd) Stock Trek/PhotoDisc; E21 Ken Karp for MMH; E22 (b) Lowell Georgia/Photo Researchers, Inc.; (tcr) Rich Treptow/Photo Researchers, Inc.; E23 (bcr) Charles D. Winters/Photo Researchers, Inc.; E23 (br) Charles D. Winters/Photo Researchers, Inc.; E23 (cr) Charles D. Winters/Photo Researchers, Inc.; E23 (cr) Russ Lappa/ Science Source/Photo Researchers, Inc.; E23 (tc) ©Science/VU/Unlimited; E23 (tr) Charles D. Winters/Photo Researchers, Inc.; E24 (bc) Yoav Levy/Phototake; E24 (bl) Bill Beatty/VU/Visuals Unlimited; E24 (br) 1998 Photodisc; E24 (cl) Charles D. Winters/Photo Researchers, Inc.; E25 (tc) David Taylor/Photo Researchers, Inc.; E25 (tl) David Taylor/Photo Researchers, Inc.; E25 (tr) David Taylor/Photo Researchers, Inc.; E26 ©Colin Cuthbert/Photo Researchers, Inc.; E28 (bcr) ©E.R. Degginger/Color-Pic, Inc.; E28 (bl) ©Charles D. Winters/Photo. Researchers, Inc.; E28 (br) Russ Lappa/Photo

R 78

Researchers, Inc.; E28 (c) Klaus Guldbrandsen/ Science Photo Library/Photo Researchers, Inc.; E28 (cl) George Bernard/Photo Researchers, Inc.; E28 (cr) Klaus Guldbrandsen/Science Photo Library/Photo Researchers, Inc.; E28 (tl) Dr. E. R. Degginger/Color-Pic, Inc.; E28 (tr) Dr. E. R. Degginger/Color-Pic, Inc.; E31 (tr) McGraw-Hill School Division; E32 (bl) Christine Coscioni/CO2, Inc.; E32 (cl) Christine Coscioni/CO2; E32 (tcr) Leonard Lessin/Peter Arnold, Inc.; E33 PhotoDisc; E34 (bkgd) ©W.Wisniewski/Okapia/Photo Researchers, Inc.; E35 Ken Karp for MMH; E36 (bc) Clyde H. Smith/Peter Arnold, Inc.; E36 (bl) Gordon Wiltsie/Peter Arnold, Inc.; E36 (br) Jeff & Alexa Henry/Peter Arnold, Inc.; E37 (cl) Cesar Llacuna/Cesar Llacuna; E37 (cr) Cesar Llacuna/Cesar Llacuna; E37 (tcr) Cesar Llacuna/Cesar Llacuna; E40 (bcr) Charles D. Winters/Photo Researchers, Inc.; E40 (br) Charles D. Winters/Photo Researchers, Inc.; E40 (c) Christine L. Coscioni/CO2, Inc.; E40 (t) Cesar Llacuna/Cesar Llacuna; E40 (tcr) ©Carolina Biological Supply/PhotoTake; E41 (b) Richard Hutchings; E41 (tcr) n/a; E42 (bl) ©Jack PlekanFundamental Photographs; E42 (tr) Richard Choy/Peter Arnold, Inc.; E42 Image Port/Index Stock; E48 (bkgd) ©Paul A. Souders/CORBIS; E50 (bkgd) ©Nathan Benn/CORBIS; E51 (br) Richard Hutchings/Hutchings; E52 (b) ©Charles D. Winters/Photo Researchers, Inc; E52 (br) Jacana/Photo Researchers, Inc.; E53 (br) ©Phil Degginger/Color-Pic, Inc.; E53 (c) ©Becky Luigart-Stayner/CORBIS; E53 (cl) ©Dr. Ed Degginger/Color-Pic, Inc.; E53 (tl) Dr. Ed Degginger/Color-Pic; E53 (tr) ©E.R. Degginger/Color-Pic, Inc.; E54 (bl) ©Phil Degginger/Color-Pic, Inc.; E54 (cr) Richard Hutchings/Hutchings; E55 (b) ©EyeWire/GETTYONE; E55 (bcr) ©Jim Corwin/Photo Researchers, Inc.; E55 (br) Phil Degginger/Color-Pic, Inc.; E55 (cr) Artville/Artville; E55 (t) ©Phil Degginger/Color-Pic, Inc.; E55 (tr) ©Phil Degginger/Color-Pic, Inc.; E56 (b) ©Phil Degginger/Color-Pic, Inc.; E56 (tr) Charles D. Winters/Photo Researchers, Inc.; E57 (tc) Richard Hutchings/Hutchings; E57 (tl) ©Richard Megna/Fundamental Photographs; E57 (tr) Richard Hutchings/Hutchings; E58 (bc) McGraw-Hill School Division; E59 (bl) Richard Hutchings/Hutchings; E59 (br) Richard Hutchings/Hutchings; E59 (tr) ©Joyce Photographics/Photo Researchers, Inc.; E60 (t) ©S. Strickland/Naturescapes/Visuals Unlimited; E61 (br) Richard Hutchings/Hutchings; E61 (cl) M.I. Walker/Photo Researchers, Inc.; E62 (bl) Hutchings/Richard Hutchings; E64 (b) ©Mark E. Gibson/VU/Visuals Unlimited; E65 (cr) ©Photodisc; E66 (c) Larry Lefever/Grant Heilman Photography, Inc.; E67 (l) David R. Frazier /Photo Researchers, Inc.; E67 (tr) ©David S. Addison/Visuals Unlimited; E68 (bkgd) ©Nik Wheeler/CORBIS; E70 (b) Richard Hutchings/Hutchings; E70 (br) Richard Hutchings/Hutchings; E70 (cr) Richard Hutchings/Hutchings; E70 (tc) Richard Hutchings/Hutchings; E70 (tr) ©Richard Hutchings/Richard Hutchings Photography; E71 (tr) Richard Hutchings/Hutchings; E72 (bl) ©Ed Degginger/Color-Pic, Inc.; E72 (br) Richard Hutchings/Hutchings; E73 (bl) ©Richard Megna/Fundamental Photographs; E73 (br) Lee Snyder/Photo Researchers, Inc.; E73 (tl) Richard Hutchings/Hutchings; E73 (tr) Richard Hutchings/Hutchings; E74 (br) NASA; E74 (tl) Christine L. Coscioni/CO2, Inc.; E74 (tl) ©Science/Visuals Unlimited; E74 (tr) Leonard Lessin/Peter Arnold, Inc.; E74 (tr) Leonard Lessin/Peter Arnold, Inc.; E75 (br) Richard Hutchings/Richard Hutchings Photograph; E76 (bl) Christine Coscioni/CO2, Inc.; E76 (tr) Cesar Llacuna/Cesar Llacuna; E77 (tr) McGraw-Hill School Division; E78 (br) ©Henry Horenstein/Stock Boston; E79 (bkgd) ©LSF OSF/Animals Animals/Earth Scenes; E79 (tl) ©Michael Newman/PhotoEdit; E80 (bkgd) ©Michael P. Gadomski/Photo Researchers, Inc.; E81 (br) McGraw-Hill School Division; E82 (bcl) ©Ken Karp/Ken Karp Photography; E82 (bcr) PhotoDisc; E82 (bl) ©Richard Megna/Fundamental Photographs; E82 (br) ©E.R. Degginger/Color-Pic, Inc.; E83 (tr) ©Kristen Brochmann/Fundamental Photographs; E84 (bl) Geoff Bryant/Photo Researchers, Inc.; E84 (br) Ken Karp/McGraw Hill School Division; E84 (cl) ©John D. Cunningham/Visuals Unlimited; E85 (br) McGraw-Hill School Division; E85 (tl) ©Renee Lynn/Photo Researchers, Inc.; E87 (br) Dan Howell/McGraw-Hill School Division; E87 (cl) Dan Howell/McGraw-Hill School Division; E87 (tl) ©Dr. E.R. Degginger/Color-Pic, Inc.; E88 (l) ©Paul Silverman/Fundamental Photographs; E89 (r) Tony Freeman/PhotoEdit; E90 (bkgd) ©Denise Mattia/Denise Mattia Underwater Photography; E91 (br) Richard Hutchings/Hutchings; E93 (b) McGraw-Hill School Division; E96 (bl) Andrew McClenaghan/Photo Researchers, Inc.; E96 (b) ©Science/Visuals Unlimited; E97 (bc) ©Michael Dalton/Fundamental Photographs; E98 (cr) Richard Hutchings/Hutchings; E99 Bettmann/CORBIS; E101 (bl) Craig Lovell/Bettmann/CORBIS;

Unit F: F0 (bkgd) Comstock; F1 (bkgd) Duomo/CORBIS; F2 (bkgd) ©PHOTRI/Tom Sanders/ THE STOCK MARKET; F4-5 (bkgd) ©Annie Griffiths Belt/CORBIS; F5 (b) McGraw-Hill School Division; F5 (cr) McGraw-Hill School Division; F6 (b) McGraw-Hill School Division; F7 (tr) ©Paul Silverman/Fundamental Photographs; F8 (b) ©Neil Rabinowitz/CORBIS; F8 (inset) ©NASA/Ed Degginger/Color-Pic, Inc.; F9 (bcr) ©Duomo/Chris Trotman/Duomo Photography Inc.; F9 (bl) ©Joe McDonald/CORBIS; F9 (tl) Museum of Flight/CORBIS; F10 (c) ©Bill Aron/Photo Researchers, Inc.; F11 (tr) ©Jerry Wachter/Photo Researchers, Inc.; F12 (tl) ©Peter Turnley/CORBIS; F13 (b) ©George Lepp/CORBIS; F13 (tr) ©Robert Mathena/Fundamental Photographs; F15 (cr) ©TSM/Photri/The Stock Market; F16-7 (bkgd) ©Ed Kashi/CORBIS; F17 (br) McGraw-Hill School Division; F17 (c) PhotoDisc/Getty Images; F17 (cr) PhotoDisc/Getty Images; F20 (tcr) ©Tony Freeman/PhotoEdit; F20 (tr) ©Ed Degginger/Color-Pic, Inc.; F21 (cr) ©Phil Degginger/Color-Pic, Inc.; F21 (tr) ©Ed Degginger/Color-Pic, Inc.; F22 (br) ©LBJ Space Center/Nasa/NASA; F25 (b) ©Kevin R. Morris/CORBIS; F25 (cl) ©Russ Schleipman/CORBIS; F25 (cr) ©Peter Turnley/CORBIS; F25 (tr) ©Paul A. Souders/CORBIS; F26 (bc) Eric Roth/FlashFocus; F26 (bl) Gregg Occo/Visuals Unlimited; F26 (br) StockByte; F26 (c) Larry Mulvehill/Photo Researchers Inc.; F26 (cl) RDF/Visuals Unlimited; F26 (cr) Walley Eberhart/Visuals Unlimited; F29 (tr) McGraw-Hill School Division; F32 (bkgd) ©Bettmann/CORBIS; F33 (br) McGraw-Hill School Division; F35 (t) ©G.Sauvage/Vandystadt/Photo Researchers, Inc.; F36 (tr) ©J-L Charmet/Science Photo Library/Photo Researchers, Inc.; F40 (bl) ©Kevin R. Morris/Corbis; F40 (tl) ©The Image Bank/Gettyone; F40 (tr) ©Davis Barber/PhotoEdit; F41 (cr) ©NASA/Media Dallas; F42-3 (b) ©ZERO/JSC/NASA; F45 (bcl) NASA/©Nasa; F46-7 (bkgd) ©Miro Vintoniv/Stock, Boston; F48-9 (bkgd) ©NASA/Galaxy Contact/Oxford Scientific Film and Photo Library; F49 (br) Richard Hutchings Photography/Richard Hutchings; F50 (bcl) Artville/Artville/PictureQuest, PhotoSpin; F50 (bcr) PictureQuest, PhotoSpin/Artville/Artville; F50 (bl) PictureQuest, PhotoSpin/Artville/Artville; F50 (br) Cartesia Software/Cartesia Software; F51 (bl) McGraw-Hill School Division; F52 (b) ©Ken Fisher/TSI/Tony Stone Images; F52 (c) PhotoDisc 2000; F53 (br) McGraw-Hill School Division; F54-5 (bkgd) ©Ulrike Welsch/Ulrike Welsch Photography; F55 (cr) Richard Hutchings/Hutchings; F56 (b) Artville LLC 1997/Artville; F56 (inset) ©Artville LLC 1997/Artville; F57 (t) Tim Davis/Photo Researchers, Inc.; F58 (bl) Courtesy Alexander Graham Bell/National Historic Park; F58 (tl) ©William James Warren/Corbis; F59 (tr) George Hall/CORBIS; F60 (t) ©1998 PhotoDisc, Inc.; F61 (c) Dr. Jeremy Burgess/Photo Researchers, Inc.; F62-3 (bkgd) Brenda Tharp/Photo Researchers, Inc.; F64-5 (bkgd) ©Kevin Fleming/CORBIS; F65 (br) Richard Hutchings/Hutchings; F66 (br) Brian Bahr/Allsport; F67 (b) ©Museum der Stadt, Vienna, Austria/Superstock; F67 (t) ©Marty Loken/Tony Stone Images/Stone; F68 (br) ©TSM/John M. Roberts/The Stock Market; F68 (cl) McGraw-Hill School Division; F69 (b) Wolfgang Kaehler/CORBIS; F72 (b) Joseph Schuyler/Stock, Boston; F72 (t) Artville; F73 (cr) Luc Novovitch/Gamma Liaison Agency; F77 (cr) PictureQuest, PhotoSpin/Artville; F77 (tr) PictureQuest, PhotoSpin/Artville; F78-9 (bkgd) ©VCG/FPG; F80-1 (bkgd) ©Richard Cummins/CORBIS; F81 (br) Richard Hutchings/Hutchings; F82 (b) Robert Holmgren/Peter Arnold, Inc.; F82 (t) ©Arthur Morris/Visuals Unlimited; F83 (bc) ©Rich Treptow/Visuals Unlimited; F83 (bcr) ©C.P. George/Visuals Unlimited; F83 (t) ©Barb Gerlach/Visuals Unlimited; F84 (br) Richard Hutchings/Hutchings; F85 (tr) Image courtesy of Barry Luokkala, Department of Physics, Carnegie Mellon University; F86 (b) Richard Hutchings/Hutchings; F87 (bl) Richard Hutchings/Hutchings; F87 (cr) Hutchings/Richard Hutchings; F87 (tr) ©Paul Silverman/Fundamental Photographs; F88 (bl) ©Roger Ressmeyer/CORBIS; F88 (inset) Roger Ressmeyer/Corbis; F88 (tc) Richard Hutchings/Hutchings; F88 (tcr) Richard Hutchings/Hutchings; F90 (tr) Cesar Llacuna/Cesar Llacuna; F91 Tony Freeman/PhotoEdit; F92 (bcr) North Wind Picture Archive/North Wind Pictures; F92 (br) Science Photo Library/Photo Researchers, Inc.; F92-3 (bkgd) Wolfgang Kaehler/CORBIS; F93 (bcr) ©Larry Mulvehill/CORBIS; F93 (br) The Schenectady Museum; F93 (br) The Queens Borough Public Library, Long Island Division,Latimer Family Papers/The Queens Borough Library/; F94-5 (bkgd) ©Jack Plekan/Fundamental Photographs; F95 (br) Richard Hutchings/Hutchings; F96 (b) Richard Hutchings/Hutchings; F96 (c) ©Alfred Pasieka/Science Photo Library/Photo Researchers, Inc.; F96 (t) ©Science/Visuals Unlimited; F97 (bcr) Richard Hutchings/Hutchings; F97 (bl) Richard Hutchings/Hutchings; F97 (t) ©Jeff Greenberg/Visuals Unlimited; F98 (bcl) Richard Hutchings/Hutchings; F98 (cl) Richard Hutchings/Hutchings; F98 (tr) ©Bill Beatty/Visuals Unlimited; F99 (bcl) Hutchings/Richard Hutchings; F99 (cl) Richard Hutchings/Hutchings; F100 (bc) Richard Hutchings/Hutchings; F100 (cr) Richard Hutchings/Hutchings; F103 (cl) ©James Webb/PhotoTake; F107 (bkgd) ©Jeremy Walker/Stone Gettyone; F107 (br) Richard Hutchings/Hutchings; F109 (br) Hutchings/Richard Hutchings Photography; F109 (tr) Hutchings/Richard Hutchings Photography; F111 (br) McGraw-Hill School Division; F113 (br) ©Ed Degginger/Color-Pic, Inc.; F114-5 (bkgd) NASA Media Dallas; F115 (br) Ken Karp for MMH; F116 (b) Richard Hutchings/Hutchings; F117 (cr) n/a; F118 (inset) Bettmann/CORBIS; F119 (bcr) ©Hewlett Packard/Fundamental Photographs; F119 (inset) ©Hewlett Packard/Fundamental Photographs; F120 (br) ©1998 PhotoDisc, Inc.; F120 (inset) ©Science/Visuals Unlimited; F121 (tr) ©Carolyn A. McKeone/Photo Researchers, Inc.; F122 (bl) ©Science/Visuals Unlimited; F123 (tr) McGraw-Hill School Division.